The Fundamental Voter

The Fundamental Voter

American Electoral Democracy, 1952–2020

JOHN H. ALDRICH
SUHYEN BAE
BAILEY K. SANDERS

OXFORD
UNIVERSITY PRESS

Oxford University Press is a department of the University of Oxford. It furthers the University's objective of excellence in research, scholarship, and education by publishing worldwide. Oxford is a registered trade mark of Oxford University Press in the UK and certain other countries.

Published in the United States of America by Oxford University Press
198 Madison Avenue, New York, NY 10016, United States of America.

© Oxford University Press 2024

All rights reserved. No part of this publication may be reproduced, stored in a retrieval system, or transmitted, in any form or by any means, without the prior permission in writing of Oxford University Press, or as expressly permitted by law, by license, or under terms agreed with the appropriate reproduction rights organization. Inquiries concerning reproduction outside the scope of the above should be sent to the Rights Department, Oxford University Press, at the address above.

You must not circulate this work in any other form
and you must impose this same condition on any acquirer.

Library of Congress Control Number: 2024936469

ISBN 978-0-19-774549-6 (pbk.)
ISBN 978-0-19-774548-9 (hbk.)

DOI: 10.1093/oso/9780197745489.001.0001

Dedicated to all principal investigators and staff who created the American National Election Studies and who maintain it as the gold standard in survey research

Contents

List of Illustrations	ix
Acknowledgments	xiii

1. A Fundamental Change in National Elections, 1952–2020   1

2. The Fundamentals: What Are They, and How Many Are There?   15

3. The Fundamentals and the Vote, 1952–2020   39

4. The Fundamentals Sort and Polarize the Electorate   62

5. How Fundamentals Shape Evaluations of Candidates and Campaigns   86

6. The Fundamentals: From Polarization to a Single Reinforced Cleavage   116

7. Conclusion   138

Notes	143
References	161
Index	169

List of Illustrations

Table

Table 5.1. Effects of Campaign-Specific Variables on Evaluations of
Candidates in 2016   102

Figures

Figure 1.1. Vote margin in presidential elections, 1952–2020   6

Figure 1.2. Incumbency advantage in US House elections, 1952–2020
(average of three measures)   7

Figure 1.3. Split seats and votes, U.S. House and presidential elections,
1952–2020   9

Figure 2.1. Apolitical individuals by race, 1952–2020   29

Figure 2.2. Democratic identifiers by race, 1952–2020   30

Figure 2.3. Comparing economic perceptions to economic reality, 1980–2020 37

Figure 3.1. Satisfaction of ideology/issue voting criteria, 1972–2020   43

Figure 3.2. Illustrating *The American Voter*'s theory of voting   45

Figure 3.3. Changing role of partisanship, issues, and candidates, 1956–1976 46

Figure 3.4. Fundamentals and their effect on presidential vote, 1988–2020 48

Figure 3.5. Fundamentals and their effect on congressional vote, 1988–2020 49

Figure 3.6. Social, economic, and demographic variables and the vote,
1972–2020   54

Figure 3.7. Fundamentals and presidential vote, 1972–2020   57

Figure 3.8. Fundamentals and congressional vote, 1972–2020   59

Figure 4.1. Partisan polarization in US House, 1879–2023   64

Figure 4.2. Forming party majority in US House, 1879–2023   65

Figure 4.3. Forming centrist majority in US House, 1879–2023   66

X LIST OF ILLUSTRATIONS

Figure 4.4.	Public's perception of party differences, 1952–2020	68
Figure 4.5.	Average of four fundamentals, 1972–2020	70
Figure 4.6.	Standard deviation of five fundamentals, 1972–2020	71
Figure 4.7.	Distribution of economic retrospection, 1980–2020	72
Figure 4.8.	Distribution of US House and public on four fundamentals, 1988 and 2020	75
Figure 4.9.	Party differences on three fundamentals	77
Figure 4.10.	Correlations among party, ideology, and issues, 1972–2020	80
Figure 4.11.	Increasing correlation among fundamentals, 1972–2020	80
Figure 4.12.	Party divergence on three fundamentals, 1972–2020	82
Figure 4.13.	Party differences on ideology in US House and public, 1972–2020	83
Figure 5.1.	Partisan evaluations of parties and presidential candidates, 1980–2020	87
Figure 5.2.	Three fundamentals, incumbency, and candidate familiarity predicting congressional vote, 1980–2020	92
Figure 5.3.	Five fundamentals, incumbency, and candidate familiarity predicting congressional vote, 1988–2020	93
Figure 5.4.	Fundamentals and evaluation of presidential nomination candidates by party, 1980 and 2016	95
Figure 5.5.	Percentage of partisans rating presidential nomination candidates of the opposing party "warmly" by party, 1980 and 2016	96
Figure 5.6.	Effect of fundamentals on Democratic candidate evaluations, 1980 and 2016	97
Figure 5.7.	Effect of fundamentals on Republican candidate evaluations, 1980 and 2016	98
Figure 5.8.	Fundamentals, election-specific factors, and the vote in 2016	102
Figure 5.9.	Partisan ratings of opposing party and opposing party candidates, 1980–2020	104
Figure 5.10.	Fundamentals and traits predicting presidential vote, 1988–2020	107
Figure 5.11.	Fundamentals, traits, and presidential vote, first differences, 1988–2020	109
Figure 5.12.	Increasing partisan differences in trait evaluations, 1984–2020	110

LIST OF ILLUSTRATIONS   xi

Figure 5.13. Path diagram of potential relationship   111

Figure 5.14. Traits as mediators, 1988–2020   111

Figure 5.1A. Baron and Kenny's mediation approach   114

Figure 5.2A. Traits as mediators of fundamentals and presidential vote   114

Figure 6.1. The Fundamentals Become Unidimensional, 1972–2020   122

Figure 6.2. Partisan sorting on issues and ideology, 1972–2020   133

Figure 6.3. Decline of crosscutting cleavages, 1972–2020   135

Figure 6.4. Comparing polarization in public and Congress, 1972–2020   136

Acknowledgments

This book has been long in the making. Over time it has transformed considerably and, we like to think, its message has grown in importance. Very many people have made intellectual contributions that appear in these pages, although they may be unaware of just how important they have been to the authors. The most important are those who have given their time and energy to making the American National Election Study (ANES) the premier election survey in the world and should be justly proud of the science they have created. We have dedicated the book to the principal investigators and the staff to reflect our and the social and behavioral scientists' debt to them. First among these are, of course, Angus Campbell, Philip E. Converse, Warren E. Miller, and Donald E. Stokes, who launched this project in the 1940s and nurtured its growth to such a premier status. In the 1970s they succeeded in having the National Science Foundation support this project from then to this day—and we hope for long into the future. The various program directors and other critical administrators have kept the ANES alive and at the forefront of the social and behavioral sciences. But there is a much larger community who have contributed to the success of the ANES. These have long been necessary components to making the ANES what it is. We thank you all.

We began with the American National Election Study (www.electionstud ies.org), of course, because its data and the scholarly accomplishments of its founders and subsequent PIs are at the very center of essentially every page in this book. We are very grateful to Duke University, Trinity College, and the Department of Political Science, which have provided research sources of many kinds, including funding and support for time for both Aldrich and Bae to conduct the research that is reported here. We want to thank Jamie L. Carson, Eric Engstrom, Gary C. Jacobson, and Jason Roberts for providing data they had acquired, even though we ended up not using all of it. Keith T. Poole and Howard Rosenthal provide their data to everyone. That includes us, but the senior author wants to offer a personal thank you to Keith, and we all are saddened by Howie's recent passing. Patrick Ramjug and Michelle Whyman made very specific and important contributions, mostly

xiv   ACKNOWLEDGMENTS

intellectual, but we would especially like to thank Patrick for coming up with the design for two of the Congress figures. We appreciate their direct and indirect help, but none of these institutions or individuals are responsible for the analyses or interpretations presented here. We three authors are solely responsible.

David McBride believed in this manuscript in ways others didn't, and he and the staff at Oxford University Press have made the book professional and attractive. We would also like to thank, in particular, Hinduja Dhanasegaran and the rest of the staff at Newgen Knowledge Works and, for her amazing work copy editing the manuscript, Sharon Langworthy. Aldrich: As always, the senior author's long colleagueship and friendship led to contributions from longtime friends and colleagues: Jim Alt, John Ferejohn, Mo Fiorina, Dave Rohde, and Ken Shepsle. There are too many to name them all, but colleagues who work on voting and elections have had up to fifty years to shape my thinking. Among those doing so recently are Leonie Huddy and Jamie Druckman, which I appreciate greatly, but there are many others. John Kessel started me on the path of my professional life and introduced me to the subject and to *The American Voter*. To the very many others who pushed me along the path to this book, I would like to express my appreciation, especially John Sullivan, Gene Borgida, Andre Blais, and, happily, so many graduate students (and a special thank you to Dave Howell). First, last, and always, it is Cindy who has made my life so fantastic.

Suhyen: I am thankful to many incredible individuals whose contributions to my academic journey and camaraderie have shaped my scholarly pursuits and developments: mentors—Okyeon Yi, Jong Hee Park, Herbert Kitschelt, Christopher D. Johnston, Candis Watts Smith; colleagues at Gross Hall, especially, Wanning Seah, Trent Ollerenshaw, Andrew Kenealy, Mateo Villamizar-Chaparro, Max Allamong; and my interdisciplinary community of like-minded scholars—Yun Ha Cho, the Book Club, and Thanksgiving buddies. Special gratitude is reserved for D. Sunshine Hillygus for her invaluable guidance on survey methodology. My deepest appreciation goes out to John Aldrich for believing in me and for his guidance and support throughout my PhD. To my family—Hyangah Kim, Seong Geun Bae, Edwin Junhyun Bae, Young Hwa Kwon, Oeok Shin, Myoungsook Bae—I extend heartfelt appreciation for their unwavering support and nourishing me with spoonfuls of love. Lastly, I would like to express my gratitude to my late grandfather Inkoo Kim, who left me with a lifetime of inspirations and a character to look up to.

Bailey: I would like to acknowledge the extraordinary debt I owe to the many people who have made it possible for me to pursue my scholarly passions: my husband, Stanislav Rabinovich; my parents, Mike and Anne Sanders; my siblings, Lindsey and John Greer; the many friends who have rooted for me along the way; and last but not least, many many thanks to John Aldrich, who provided steadfast support as I pursued my PhD and JD.

1
A Fundamental Change in National Elections, 1952–2020

Every election is unique. Recent contests—from the "hanging chads" of the Bush-Gore contest in 2000, to electing the first African American president in 2008, to the incredibly nasty Clinton-Trump campaigns in 2016, to the "Big Lie" about electoral fraud that Donald J. Trump promulgated even before Election Day in 2020—demonstrate that there are unique features to every election. And it is not just the presidential races. Even midterm congressional campaigns seem to differ from each other, like the big Democratic victory to capture a congressional majority in 2006 and an even larger reversal in 2010, giving the Republicans a huge victory. The Republicans extended that victory in 2014 with very low turnout, being successful simply because it was those relatively few voters who turned out and preferred the Republicans to the Democrats. That majority was reversed again in 2018, but this time with very high turnout. The tables turned once more with a Republican majority in the US House of Representatives in 2022 but with a surprisingly small and limited victory, instead of the "red wave" many had forecast.

While there is no denying that every election has its unique aspects, the message of this book is that recent elections should be understood primarily as the result of a nearly continuously increasing set of electoral trends that began in the mid-1980s. The 1984 elections in particular mark a turning point in national elections. On one side of 1984 was a forty-year run of one form of elections, as discussed below, while the new current form appeared on the other side of 1984. Thus, one lesson of this book is that voters, in many very important senses, are consistent in their views and choices, a consistency that is measured generationally rather than quadrennially.

The ongoing march since 1984, however, has another incredibly important feature. The structure of American public opinion and voting behavior is shaped by the continuous movement toward a singular, reinforced cleavage, one that is both broadening and deepening, election after election. So serious

The Fundamental Voter. John H. Aldrich, Suhyen Bae, and Bailey K. Sanders, Oxford University Press.
© Oxford University Press 2024. DOI: 10.1093/oso/9780197745489.003.0001

2 THE FUNDAMENTAL VOTER

is the strength of this cleavage, there is reason to believe that even if Trump had not resorted to his Big Lie in 2020, electoral democracy itself would nonetheless be under threat. This cleavage, in other words, is so broad and so deep—and by now, so lasting—that it threatens the public's views of the legitimacy of elections and thus of American democracy itself. It is a partisan division—and much more than that—that cleaves our public and its government into nearly equal and opposed halves.

We seek to demonstrate the empirical veracity of these claims in what follows. In the rest of this chapter, we show that elections from 1952 (when our data start) through 1984, despite their unique aspects, had important similarities that defined that democratic era. Elections changed in 1984, with both parties now able to win majorities in the Electoral College, in the House, and in the Senate. The special additional feature of post-1984 electoral politics is that House and presidential contests are converging toward each other.[1] Many refer to that as the "nationalization" of congressional elections, which we believe to be apt, but it also represents the commonality of public behavior in contemporary American elections, regardless of office.

We next turn to what we (not originally) call the "fundamentals" of electoral choice. We will show that they are of growing importance in determining how the public votes for Congress and for president. These fundamentals' growing importance in both contests explains, we believe, why the post-1984 trend is marked by this consistent drive toward an even, 50–50 balance between the two parties. Their increasing significance in both House and presidential elections also explains why these two contests are converging; that is, both are nationalizing, by which we mean they are relying less on the specific features of the contenders and more on the fundamental forces in electoral politics. Finally, we will show not only how these fundamentals have a partisan component, but also how the institutional structure of elections funnels them through partisanship in our two-party system. As all of the fundamentals increase in potency in accounting for voters' choices, the partisan funnel through which the fundamentals necessarily flow increases in importance as well.

This growing importance of the various fundamentals is one part of what we mean by a broadening of the partisan cleavage that increasingly defines American electoral politics. The second part of this broadening is that the various cleavages are changing, step by step, from being crosscutting to reinforcing one another. In this sense electoral polarization is less the growing extremisms of the public than it is the broadening of the elements that go into shaping the partisan cleavage. Elites may well be seen as "polarizing" in the sense of becoming ever more extreme in their views. The public, however, has tended to move very modestly toward extreme positions from the moderate views on issues, economics, race, and ideology that have long characterized them—and still largely do. Instead, all of the fundamentals have increasingly come into alignment with one another, a phenomenon some refer to as "party sorting" (e.g., Fiorina 2017). The reinforcement of the various elements of this increasingly potent and substantive partisan cleavage is one reason to worry about American electoral politics today. Before 1984, it was common to see the Democrats as standing near the typical voter on some important matters and the Republicans as standing closer on others. Now, even if the voter is indeed only moderately liberal (or conservative), they look at the Republicans (or at the Democrats) and see that they stand on the other side of the divide on nearly everything of importance to them in politics.

The second reason is the final step in our argument. It is that the breadth of elements brought together in the partisan cleavage is related to (and likely preceded) the growing emotional reaction to this increasingly broad partisan cleavage. As we will see, it seems to matter less to the public that their party has become increasingly aligned on the fundamentals with their own views. Rather, what is important is that the opposition is ever more consistently on the wrong side of every important aspect of politics. Finding the opposition on the wrong side of nearly everything of importance, we believe, generates negative emotion, and the growing negativity (often referred to as "affective partisanship," wherein the affect is invariably negative) leads to very negative assessments of the other party and the other party's candidates (e.g., Iyengar et al. 2019). This deepening of negative affect goes hand in hand with the broadening of the cleavage to make the divide in US politics increasingly seem unbridgeable. Adding increasingly high levels of negative affect to politically substantive reinforcement of the fundamentals creates a serious threat to the stability of the US political system. To be sure, the electorate is not the only source of polarization and negativity in US politics. But in a republican democracy, as Madison put it in *Federalist* No. 10, all power flows directly or indirectly from the great body of the people (Hamilton, Maddison, and Jay 1961). Their dislike of, perhaps hatred for or even disgust with, the opposing half of America is what makes America today once again a house divided and perhaps increasingly close to being unable to stand.

4 THE FUNDAMENTAL VOTER

The Evolution of Presidential and Congressional Elections

We begin with our claim that American national elections in the post–World War II era are divided into two groups, those before and those after 1984. Elections in both of these groups have stark similarities to each other but differ from those in the other group. Before 1984 presidential contests were predominantly determined by party loyalties and the characteristics of the two candidates, and this appeared to be largely true in each contest from 1952 (when our data start) to 1984. Congressional contests, by contrast, began by being apparently dominated strictly by party loyalties, with only a small role for the influence of the candidates. Over time the importance of the candidates increased, especially the role played by incumbents seeking re-election. Beginning in or around 1984, presidential contests became increasingly close races between the two parties, and any influence of the candidates, even of incumbents, which once loomed so large, has on net receded. So, too, on the congressional side has the influence of incumbency waned to the quite small role it played, on average, in the 1950s. What is important (as we will show in subsequent chapters) is the increasing role of a diverse set of what we call fundamentals shaping electoral choice. And it is this growth of importance of fundamentals that has led to the convergence of presidential and congressional votes.

Let's begin with presidential elections. In the middle of the twentieth century, political scientists had a theoretical puzzle to unravel. Scholars such as Angus Campbell, Philip E. Converse, Warren E. Miller, and Donald E. Stokes (especially in 1960) argued that party identification was the single dominant long-term force, anchoring and structuring the public's views on all of the short-term considerations that spring up from election to election. Yet although the electorate was anywhere from 55–45 to 60–40 for Democrats in their "normal vote" (which is to say their partisan vote; Converse 2006), the 1952 and 1956 presidential elections resulted in Republican victories—and one was by a landslide. Even when the Republican candidate lost in 1960, it was by one of the smallest margins in American history. Partisanship appeared to structure what the public knew and thought about electoral politics, but it did not seem to shape the outcome. Subsequent elections revealed another paradox of partisan-centered elections. Party identification changed very little over time; it was its long-term durability that made it such a fundamental fact about American elections. And yet that nearly unchanging force, tilted noticeably in a Democratic direction, was associated not only with Republican victories in the 1950s but also with wild swings from one election to the next. Swings went from very close nail-biters (e.g., in 1960 and 1968), to massive landslides (in 1964 and 1972), and then back again to an extremely close race (1976). How could an electorate predisposed to be Democratic, with more citizens than not viewing the world through a Democratic lens, not only elect Republicans so often but also be so changeable in their net votes as to gyrate the outcome between razor-thin victories and massive landslides?

Stokes (1966) proposed an answer: partisanship, he believed, still provided that long-term, durable structuring principle for understanding politics, but it was the short-term features of the election, and in particular the qualities of the two presidential candidates, that provided the dynamics of particular elections. The electorate may have been more Democratic than Republican, but the individual traits of presidential candidates could lead voters to choose a candidate from the opposing party. And if that winning candidate had a good four-year term, the opposition might well flock to his side, giving him a landslide victory, whether Republican or Democrat. That is, over the long run a voter might tend to choose the Democratic (Republican) candidate, but he or she also responded to the particular characteristics of a given electoral contest, especially the characteristics of the two major-party contenders. Voting across party lines was not just possible; it was commonplace.

This characterization of voters and presidential elections, however, no longer appears to be accurate. Figure 1.1 reports the margin of victory for the winning presidential candidate, that is, the percent of the popular vote won by the leading candidate less that of the other party's nominee over the entire American National Election Study (ANES) survey period (from 1952 to 2020). If we were to divide that figure in two, there is a strong case for choosing 1984 as the point of division. From 1952 through 1984, the presidential vote gyrated from close contests to landslide victories and back to razor-thin margins again, nearly from election to election. It is very much a sawtooth pattern, one with very large teeth.

From 1984 onward the vote margins flatten out, losing their sawtooth-like aspect, and the margin of victory appears to be declining inexorably toward a 50–50 division between votes for the Democratic and Republican candidates. Whether the election features an incumbent (1992, 1996, 2004, 2012, and 2020) or two nonincumbent candidates (1988, 2000, 2008, and 2016), this is an era with no landslide elections. As we will see, this is because voting

6 THE FUNDAMENTAL VOTER

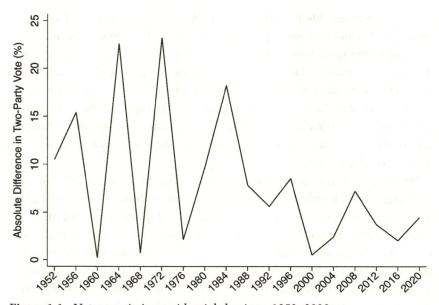

Figure 1.1. Vote margin in presidential elections, 1952–2020
Source: Compiled by authors. Data from Gerhard Peters, "Presidential Election Margins of Victory," The American Presidency Project, 1999–2021, https://www.presidency.ucsb.edu/node/323891.

has become increasingly driven by fundamentals, and the typical voter is increasingly found on their party's side of each fundamental.

This appears to be a dramatic change. One way we can quantify that change is to consider the standard deviation of the victory margins. From 1952 through 1984, the standard deviation of the victory margins shown in Figure 1.1 was 9.1. From 1988 through 2020, it was just under 3.0. Another way to quantify the change in victory margins over time is to consider the correlation of the vote margin with time. Visually, it appears that there is little time trend before 1984 and a very large time trend thereafter, and the correlations confirm this suspicion. The correlation of the presidential vote over the years from 1952 to 1984 is only +.09, whereas from 1984 on it is −.64.[2]

What Figure 1.1 seems to suggest is that there is no longer much of an incumbency advantage for presidents seeking re-election; the ability to enter a second term of office on the wave of a landslide election seems unlikely no matter who is seeking a second term. Even William J. "Bill" Clinton, whose public approval ratings hovered in the 50 and 60 percents on the eve of the 1996 election, about as high as any incumbent in the post-1984 period, beat Robert J. Dole by only nine percentage points, and that was the largest margin in the new era, though one of the smallest of the easy victories in the earlier era.

The next question to consider, then, is whether this is also true for congressional elections. Studies of congressional elections in the 1970s and 1980s provided justification for Speaker of the U.S. House Thomas P. "Tip" O'Neill, Jr. aphorism that "all politics is local," or at least that congressional elections were rooted in the particularities of the individual congressional district.[3] What mattered was what the district was like, who the candidates were, and how the electorate matched up with and evaluated those candidates. And among these district-specific items, one question was much more important than any other: Was there an incumbent running for re-election? It appeared that virtually all incumbents were capable of exploiting their office to get a larger and larger edge over any challenger such that national politics, party platforms, and the like could matter, but only as they were reflected through the prism of the specific candidates and by the particular makeup of the district.

Gary Jacobson (esp. 2015) has shown that congressional politics is no longer "personal" (as he calls it) but is increasingly reflective of national politics. As Figure 1.2 demonstrates, the same "change" that occurred in presidential elections has a counterpart in congressional elections. Figure 1.2 reports the average of three measures political scientists have developed to assess the incumbency advantage.[4] As the figure shows, incumbency brought very little

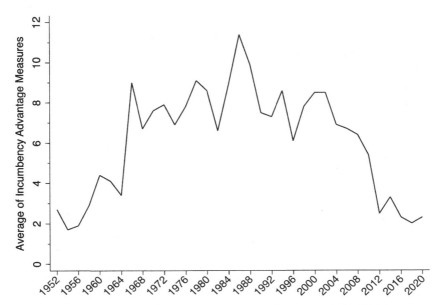

Figure 1.2. Incumbency advantage in US House elections, 1952–2020 (average of three measures)

Source: Compiled by authors. Data provided by Gary C. Jacobson and Jamie L. Carson percomm. 2/7/2022.

8 THE FUNDAMENTAL VOTER

electoral advantage, usually fewer than three points, in the 1950s. That advantage increased substantially in the 1960s to about 2000, when it ranged from 6 to 12 percent. It peaked around 1984 and began to decline, especially following the Clinton years, such that it was 2 to 3 percent in the last three elections. To reinforce the visual indication of increasing advantage with time through 1984 followed by declining advantage, the correlation with time from 1952 through 1984 is +.85, meaning that incumbency advantage was increasing year after year, while it is −.88, or decreasing in every election, thereafter.

This evidence suggests a third factor of considerable importance for understanding American elections: a growing convergence between presidential and congressional elections. Incumbency mostly was what led to the sawtooth shape of presidential outcomes through 1984, depending primarily on whether there was an incumbent or not, but the incumbency advantage in presidential elections appears to have declined since then.[5] The importance of incumbency per se also appears to have risen and then declined in the House. If the most prominent candidate-specific feature of both elections, the value of being an incumbent, has declined in the last forty years, that suggests that partisanship and other forces, the rest of our fundamentals, are making the two sets of national elections increasingly similar.

Figure 1.3 supports Jacobson's (2015) findings on this point as well; it reports the number of House seats won by a candidate whose partisan affiliation differed from that of the presidential candidate who won the district. These "split" districts peaked in 1984 at 45 percent of all House seats. In other words, at least during the (rather regularly occurring) landslide elections years, like 1972 and 1984, it was close to a coin toss whether the party's presidential and House candidates would both carry the district.[6] The percentage then declined, almost consistently, to 6 percent in 2012, 8 percent in 2016, and just under 4 percent in 2020. That is to say, almost half the seats were split in the 1980s, but less than one in ten is now.

The percentage of voters who report casting a split ticket—that is, voting for one party for president and the other party for the House—increased almost continuously from 1952 to 1972. Reported split-ticket voting then began to decline almost continuously from 1972 (30 percent) and 1980 (28 percent) to 2020 (11 percent), as Figure 1.3 also shows. Just like the incumbency advantage, split-ticket voting has declined back to where it started from two generations ago. Further, the rise in casting split tickets through 1984 and its decline thereafter are stark. For the aggregate measure of split districts, the correlation between the incidence of split districts and time is +.71 through 1984 and −.93 thereafter. For reported percentages of casting split-ticket votes, the comparable correlations are +.86 and −0.91, respectively.

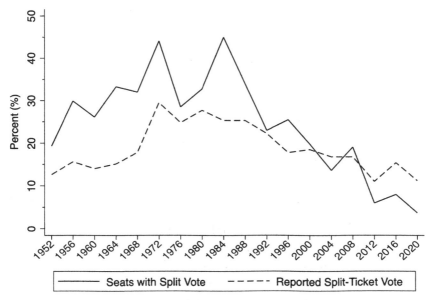

Figure 1.3. Split seats and votes, U.S. House and presidential elections, 1952–2020

Source: Compiled by authors. Data provided by Gary Jacobson and Jamie Carson percomm. ANES Guide https://electionstudies.org/data-tools/anes-guide/anes-guide.html?chart=split_ticket_voting

That both congressional and presidential elections have changed—and that congressional elections are in closer alignment with the presidential vote—provides a strong, if preliminary, basis for making the inference that voters choose their respective candidates based on the same factors in both settings. Indeed, we suggest that the common factors driving voter choice in both presidential and congressional elections can be thought of as the *fundamentals* of electoral choice. As we will show, these fundamental factors of electoral choice explain congressional electoral choices just about as well as presidential electoral choices—and that is very well indeed.

The Road to Come

In the following chapters we will develop the notion of fundamentals more fully and precisely. We begin to do so in Chapter 2, where we first define the criteria we use to determine if a candidate factor can be considered to be a fundamental. As Campbell et al. (1960) said about party identification, it is a durable and commonly held force that serves to orient the public to

10 THE FUNDAMENTAL VOTER

electoral politics. We extend that consideration to four other fundamentals—
ideology, recurring issues, race, and economic assessments. In Chapter 2 we
focus on the importance that scholars have associated with each of these five
fundamentals, their enduring nature, and the role they have played in scholarly theories about public opinion and voting behavior. In Chapter 3 we continue this assessment by showing that each has a substantive political basis,
rather than an ephemeral one, and that each is commonly closely associated
with the vote. We conclude by demonstrating how much more strongly these
five fundamentals have oriented the citizen to politics and thus helped shape
their electoral choices.

Perhaps the most common current description of partisan politics
today is that it is deeply polarized. While we do not study the politics of
Congress closely in this book, we follow the dominant interpretation of
what most mean by partisan polarization in Congress. The claim, and
much readily available evidence, is understood as showing that Democrats
and Republicans in Congress are increasingly divided into two partisan
camps; the divide is widening as the parties appear to be moving toward
their respective extremes; and as commonality is shunted to the side, negative and hostile outbursts are increasingly common. These are of course
very important developments. We show in Chapter 4 that the electorate
has its own form of polarization. The public has not become much more
extreme in its views, overall. Most in the public are moderates. They may
be on the left or right side of many things, but they are only modestly on
one side. What is important, however, is that the public has gone from
most individuals having some liberal and some conservative views to being
what some (e.g., Fiorina 2017) call "sorted"; that is, they now have moderately liberal-Democratic views about almost everything or moderately
conservative-Republican views about almost everything. This, as we show,
has driven a wedge between most Democrats and most Republicans. In this
sense, the parties in the electorate are more polarized from each other.

In Chapter 5 we look at what many consider to be a major consequence of
partisan polarization. Politics today, in Washington, D.C., in state capitals,
and now more often in the home, is increasingly hostile, angry, and threatening. Indeed, too often it has become violent. The rise in negative emotions,
revealed in our context by what Iyengar and others call "affective partisanship" (where the affect is invariably negative; see, e.g., Iyengar et al. 2019), is
basically a product of this millennium. It thus seems to follow the increase
in partisan polarization in Congress by years if not even a full generation. It

follows the changes in voting we outlined earlier in the chapter by a decade and more. It follows the sorting of electoral polarization. It thus appears to be in large part a consequence of these various changes. For our part, we do not believe that one can separate the more cognitive substance of politics from the more emotional affective components of political attitudes and beliefs. While we do look to see how we might understand emotional assessments of candidates as mediating the role of the fundamentals, we do so less in a sense of there being a one-way attribution of cause and effect and more on an understanding of how the long-term role of fundamentals helps orient the voter to the short-term assessments of the presidential candidates. In this sense, our work may be seen as a contemporary variant of Stokes's (1966) analysis of party identification and candidate evaluations.

In the last substantive chapter we address a more historical, comparative, and philosophic question, the role of cleavages in supporting or undermining the stability of democratic institutions. James Madison argued in *Federalist* No. 10 for the importance of moving from a state-centered to a more national-focused government, on the grounds that such an "extended republic" would be dominated by crosscutting cleavages. Doing so would thereby reduce the possibility of tyranny by an enduring majority. Seymour Martin Lipset and Stein Rokkan (1967a, b) focused attention on the importance of often historically rooted cleavages for understanding the stability of democratic institutions. Their work dominated comparative study of democracies for decades, with a central idea being that a single, dominant cleavage threatened democratic stability. We show that the incidence of crosscutting cleavages among our fundamentals has declined precipitously in recent years, as a single broadening, deepening cleavage has come to dominate electoral politics and choices.

We employ data from numerous sources, but we rely very heavily on survey data from the ANES. We do so for two reasons. First, if we want to understand and make inferences about the public, or the electorate as a whole, there is no substitute for a well-crafted survey to do so, and the ANES is arguably the best survey in the world. Second, the ANES has been conducting presidential-year surveys since 1952, and it has a very well-developed tradition of asking many of the same questions about the same core concepts over long periods of time—some reaching all the way back to 1952, many to 1972, and the rest that we will be featuring beginning in the 1980s—thus allowing us to trace the evolution of voter opinion and the vote, especially in the new era that appears to have begun in 1984.

12 THE FUNDAMENTAL VOTER

Surveys came under heavy scrutiny in 2016, as they appeared to have missed Trump's electoral vote victory and certainly led media analysts and pundits astray in their high level of confidence that Clinton would win.[7] In the academy, the "causal revolution" in the social and behavioral sciences has emphasized other limitations to survey-based inferences. While the ANES performed especially well in 2016 in particular, such that respondents reported intentions and actual votes that were very close to the national result, the strengths of the ANES lie more in its unusually high-quality (often referred to as being the "gold standard") of surveys[8] and the simple fact that high-quality national surveys have strengths that no other method, including those employed in the causal revolution, can touch. No other method can make sound, scientifically justified inferences about the national electorate and how voters choose.

The idea that the strengthening and reinforcing nature of the fundamentals narrows the ability of the candidates and their campaigns to change people's minds about whom they will support in the election does not mean that the fundamentals are set in stone. Our belief is that these conclusions are the consequences of the nature of our electoral and party system today. In large measure (and in shorthand summary here), party lines are drawn firmly and set the limits of possible outcomes well in advance of the campaigns. But those party lines are not immovable. Indeed, as we argue in the following chapters, the Trump presidency might turn out to have ushered in a new era that may redefine the parties and the existing nature of the currently reinforcing cleavages. The strengthening and reinforcing nature of the fundamentals also means that the American polity is approximating ever more closely a single, deeply divided electorate through this reinforced cleavage, and this approaching circumstance raises the specter of normative concerns that have shaped our understanding of deeply divided democracies so powerfully.

Appendix 1A Why Surveys?

While we use a variety of different kinds of data to make the case we have outlined here, by far our major source of data is a series of national surveys conducted by the American National Election Study. Surveys became controversial in 2016, being accused of "getting the election wrong." So let us take a few paragraphs to explain why we use surveys, why indeed they are by far the best and most appropriate source of data for the study of national electorates and of the functioning of electoral democracy in America.

First, to allay the concern that "surveys got it wrong" in 2016, that year was actually one of the best for *national* election surveys. They were especially accurate in getting the popular vote nationwide between Clinton and Trump very close to right.[9] As for the survey we use, the ANES reported voting of 53 percent Clinton to 46 percent Trump (in the face-to-face sample) or 52 percent to 47 percent (in the web sample) was very close to the actual outcome of 51.1 percent for Clinton to 48.9 percent for Trump.

Second, we use surveys because they are unique in being able to make inferences about what the national electorate thought, believed, and did. No other data allow us to look at what voters valued and how they decided, starting with the individual responses of single voters and faithfully aggregating all the way up to what the national public valued and how the national electorate decided. There are limits to what we can conclude from surveys, of course, but they alone can allow us to study the pulse of the nation as a whole.

Third, the ANES is unquestionably the highest quality survey of the national electorate—period. The ANES was the first national academic survey. It began to study the national electorate in 1948 and did its first full, wide-ranging interviews in 1952. It has conducted a presidential election survey every election since then (and numerous other surveys as well). It is designed to reflect the concerns of political, social, and behavioral scientists generally and thus has among the broadest coverage of opinions, values, and beliefs among the public. It has been supported continuously by the National Science Foundation (NSF) since 1978, and that support is conditioned on mounting a survey that serves the interests of the academy and the general public more generally.[10]

There are several reasons the ANES has been called the "gold standard" in survey research.[11] Central among these is that this survey has the highest standards in sampling. Many surveys today are online surveys that gather their participants from those who choose to "opt in" to respond to the survey. Some of these are very fine surveys, carefully conducted. The procedures involved nonetheless induce biases, especially those that arise from an interest in politics, due precisely to their opt-in nature. Those who choose to opt in differ from those who do not in ways that are often quite relevant for understanding their political beliefs and behaviors. To be sure, there are ways to attempt to ameliorate such biases, but such corrections are often incomplete, especially in terms of studying the sorts of preferences and beliefs of most interest for understanding voting behavior.[12]

Further, the (scientifically proper) use of a sample drawn specifically for the survey at hand has a rigorous statistical-scientific basis for making inferences from the sample to the population. This is critical because no matter how it is actually done, a survey not based on pure randomized sampling for the purposes of that particular survey does not have such a scientific basis. Indeed, this is one of the foundations of the "gold standard" designation for the ANES—the highest quality standards to ensure the best available ability to make inferences about the national electorate.[13]

The second major feature we exploit here that contributes to the "gold standard" status of the ANES surveys is their continuity. As noted, there have been full surveys of the national electorate every four years since 1952. The ANES pays a great deal of attention to striking a balance between the newest innovations in survey questions and continuing measurement of core concepts. Here we exploit the continuity of the "time series." What we have been calling the "fundamentals" (and which we will describe in more detail in later chapters) are questions that have proved their worth and that the ANES has asked in identical or nearly identical ways over long periods of time. In our case, we will make extended comparisons over time, comparing 2020 to elections extending back to 1988 in fullest detail, 1980 in rather full detail (a useful base year, in that it was the election that

14 THE FUNDAMENTAL VOTER

began the partisan polarization of recent decades), and in some cases back to 1972 (which combines a longer run of relatively low levels of partisan polarization with a beginning year in which there were some important innovations in the survey instrument).

Appendix 1B A Note on Graphical Presentations

Much of our evidence can be displayed graphically. We are especially interested in how our findings have evolved over the last generation or even two generations. If, say, the ability of our fundamentals to predict the vote can, in principle, vary from 0 to 100 percent but realistically varies from about 70 to 100 percent, the visual presentation of the steepness or dramatic ups and downs of such changes looks much different if the y axis includes the full 100 point range or "only" the realistic range of 30 or so points. Of course changing the scale of the y axis only changes how it looks, not what the data show. To that end, we provide one view (often of the more realistic, but smaller, range of variation) in the text. In the online appendix we include another version of the figures with the full range of variation possible on the y axis.[14] More importantly, we also present the data themselves, so that readers can see not only the two figures but also the actual numbers that underlie them.

2

The Fundamentals

What Are They, and How Many Are There?

In 1952 Dwight D. Eisenhower was elected president as a Republican, and his party won majorities in both the House and Senate. But then, only two years later, Democrats won back a majority of seats in the two chambers. They kept those majorities in 1956, in spite of the Republicans holding the White House in a landslide re-election. The Democrats held onto their majority in the Senate until 1981 and in the House all the way to 1995. Forty years of control of the House is by far the longest such period in American history. This decades-long control of the chambers of Congress seemed to reflect the then newly discovered fact that more people claimed to think of themselves as Democrats than identified as Republicans. Moreover, this balance favoring Democrats was true in nearly every national survey since polling began at the height of the New Deal, and it continues to this day.[1] Analyzing the first national election studies (American National Election Study, ANES), Campbell et al. (1960) gave party identification pride of place, and later on they claimed that voting for Congress was primarily an expression of partisanship (Stokes and Miller 1962).[2] Presidential elections, on the other hand, were different. *The American Voter* was based on data from two Republican presidential victories, one a substantial landslide. While Ike was unique in being a heroic World War II general who had been wooed by both parties in 1952, his vice president, Richard M. Nixon, was chosen for that post in part because of his highly charged partisan behavior. And yet he essentially tied with John F. Kennedy, the Democrat, in 1960 and virtually tied again in 1968 when he defeated Hubert H. Humphrey (Democrat) and George C. Wallace (American Independent Party). Those narrow races were, for him, but a prelude to his historic landslide re-election victory over Senator George S. McGovern (D-SD) in 1972. Clearly having more partisan identifiers is not the same thing as winning elections.

The pride of place that the authors of *The American Voter* gave to party identification was not because it determined the vote but because it was

---

The Fundamental Voter. John H. Aldrich, Suhyen Bae, and Bailey K. Sanders, Oxford University Press.
© Oxford University Press 2024. DOI: 10.1093/oso/9780197745489.003.0002

16 THE FUNDAMENTAL VOTER

the fundamental force that oriented the public to politics and especially to elections. A large majority reported a partisan attachment, typically formed early in life, often well before reaching voting age. Once formed, this preference was durable, changing only in response to dramatic upheavals in personal or political conditions. It shaped—but did not determine—how many people came to understand politics. They tended to view events through partisan eyes and reacted to events in partisan terms, for example often evaluating their party's candidates more highly than those of the opposition. While Campbell et al. (1960) referred to partisanship as a "long-term force," we find the term *fundamental force* even more descriptive.[3]

Party identification was the fundamental force in the 1950s, and it is still a fundamental force in the 2020s. From that fixed point, however, there have been two major developments, both starting in the 1980s. Party identification was effectively the only fundamental force for most of the public in the 1950s, but today several others have emerged that help a large proportion of voters orient themselves to politics. The second development is that the newly emergent fundamentals began as reasonably separate, distinct factors as the 1980s opened, but since then they have come increasingly to overlap. This last point is called "sorting" by some (e.g., Fiorina 2017). As we will see, this sorting process is the primary way in which the electorate has polarized along party lines, rather than taking on more extreme opinions on issues or other matters of substance about politics.[4] What this means is that increasingly, all fundamentals point in the same direction, an evolution with serious consequences. A relatively benign one is that this process explains the electoral transformations discussed in the previous chapter that began in the 1980s and continue today.

A more serious consequence is electoral cleavages and their role in stabilizing democracy. James Madison, in his famous *Federalist* No. 10 (Hamilton, Madison, and Jay 1961), argued that a major reason to empower a national government through the Constitution, rather than having stronger states and a weaker national government as existed under the Articles of Confederation, was that by "extending the sphere" of the nation, a larger variety of interests would motivate political actors. It would thus be far less likely that such multitudinous interests could coalesce to form a permanent majority that would act in a manner averse "to the rights of other citizens, or to the permanent and aggregate interests of the community," as Madison defined tyranny.[5] In today's language, there would be many crosscutting cleavages. Sorting, however, has been involved in an aligning of the numerous cleavages from their being primarily crosscutting to becoming increasingly reinforcing cleavages, almost as if all were essentially one large (or as we refer to it, broad and deep) electoral cleavage. And as many scholars have argued, when reinforcing cleavages approximate a single, deep cleavage, Madison's advantage for the extended sphere is lost and the ability of a democracy to survive is seriously threatened (discussed in detail in Chapter 6).

This chapter and those that follow make the case for what we mean by a fundamental force and for the current polity to best be described as having several such fundamentals. We then turn to show that these are each increasingly potent for understanding the public's political opinions and behavior. We further demonstrate their transition from mostly crosscutting to increasingly reinforcing lines of cleavage. Finally, we show that the path is leading toward, if it has not already reached, a sufficiently singular and deep line of cleavage as to threaten the continuation of America's republican democracy. We begin by considering what forces shape citizens' voting choices.

Social Context of the Vote

In the 1940s, social and behavioral scientists at Columbia University conducted surveys in two small cities to study presidential elections (Lazarsfeld, Berelson, and Gaudet [1948] 1968; Berelson, Lazarsfeld, and McPhee [1954] 1986).[6] They were interested in many topics, but especially in political communications, such as how candidates might be able to use advertising and propaganda in the then-new media of mass communications to shape their electoral fortunes. The researchers discovered that many in the public had made up their minds well before the general election campaign had even begun. Of course, Franklin D. Roosevelt was campaigning for his third and fourth terms and was probably the best known person in America. But their data also revealed the importance of social, economic, and demographic settings for shaping these preliminary and often final choices. To paraphrase, they found that people act politically as they exist socially. Income, education, occupation, and religion were the important components of their "index of political predispositions."[7] These factors reflected the structure of the New Deal coalition Roosevelt had built, and class and religious identities were (and are) structurally stable for many, so their conclusion that these predispositions translated into choices without needing to know much about candidates or issues of the moment seemed

18 THE FUNDAMENTAL VOTER

quite plausible.[8] Indeed, the way journalists, scholars, and the general public described the New Deal Democratic coalition was precisely based on these kinds of characteristics: the "working man," Catholics, urban residents, and so on, rather than, say, liberals or conservatives, pro-choice or pro-life, which we use today as part of our definition of contemporary partisan coalitions. Of course it is important to remember that we still use socioeconomic and racial-ethnic categories to complete the partisan picture.

Campbell et al. (1960) began their monumental work by acknowledging the massive contributions that Paul F. Lazarsfeld and his collaborators hade made. Indeed, seven chapters in *The American Voter* are devoted to the social and economic context of the study, one more than they devoted to the political context of issues, candidates, and partisanship. Just because someone was in the working class, a Catholic, or today, an African American, however, does not tell us *why* they were predisposed to support Democrats. In between the social and economic characteristics of the voters and their candidate choices in the election were the political orientations that translated the Columbia school's predispositions into intentions and then behavior. These psychological orientations that connected predispositions with voting behavior were Campbell et al.'s (1960) answer to the scientific question: Why? They noted that six proximal attitudes—toward the two candidates, toward political parties and other politically oriented groups, and toward domestic and international issues—were the "short-term attitudes" of the immediate election. But these short-term attitudes also did not give a satisfactory answer to why someone voted as they did. These attitudes were just too close to the vote, virtually equivalent to saying people voted for Eisenhower because they liked him (and, indeed, "I like Ike" was his campaign slogan). The connective tissue between remote and largely unvarying class, race, religion, and so on and the short-term, immediately proximate attitudes was the key psychological orientations, the long-term forces that we call the *fundamentals*.

The theory Campbell and colleagues proposed is that socioeconomic and other contextual forces set the background. Long-term psychological forces carry those predispositions into politically relevant forces for orienting the voters to the electoral system and structure how the voters take in and evaluate the specific features of the candidates, parties, and issues; this in turn leads to their choices. The authors' account is very close to our own. Later on we will specify what our socioeconomic background measures are, but here we amplify and extend the theory started by Campbell et al. (1960) to explain the increasingly rich and polarized political world of the twenty-first century. That is, we focus on the fundamental forces of electoral politics.

The Fundamentals

What *is* a fundamental?[9] As noted earlier, Campbell et al.'s (1960; see also Converse 2006) approach was to focus on electoral forces with an enduring relevance to politics for many people and that tend to change slowly over time, if at all. They pointed to party identification and ideology as the two most likely long-term forces to meet their definition.[10] We, in turn, propose an expansion of that number to five fundamentals of electoral choice, based on four criteria:

1. The fundamental is an enduring feature of American electoral politics.
2. The fundamental does not depend upon the identity of the candidates for its meaning or else depends only to a limited degree upon the specific circumstances of the particular election.
3. The fundamental is close to the center of some reasonably well-developed theory about electoral politics (and thus the scholarly community has advocated for the theoretical and empirical importance of this fundamental).
4. The fundamental is typically strongly connected empirically to voters' decision-making and their choices.[11]

We take as one piece of evidence of any potential fundamental's durability (and one nearly necessary condition to show its enduring relevance to elections) that the ANES has determined it is a "core" measure, such that it is included in (almost) every survey since its measures were first implemented. Party identification, for example, has been asked about in essentially the same form since the beginning of the ANES, and the seven-point ideology and some similarly measured seven-point issue scales have been included since they were first asked about in that form in 1972.[12]

As to the second characteristic, focusing on items that are typically strongly correlated with the vote means that some regularly included ANES batteries—such as political interest and authoritarianism—while certainly important for many purposes, do not qualify as fundamentals of voting behavior because they are often not closely related to candidate choice. If, as

20   THE FUNDAMENTAL VOTER

perhaps has happened recently with authoritarianism, a variable is related strongly to the vote in specific electoral contexts, that is because of the individual peculiarities of candidates, context, or concerns of that election.

The third criterion admittedly has a degree of ambiguity. Few potential fundamentals are really immune from being influenced by short-term considerations, as a debate over party identification has illustrated (e.g., Erikson et al. 2002; Green et al. 2002). However, for some fundamentals the direction of influence is sufficiently one-sided as to say that they are substantially more influential in affecting truly short-term considerations than the reverse.[13]

Much of this chapter is devoted to assessing the first two criteria, while Chapter 3 looks at the third and fourth criteria. We believe five measures meet these criteria: partisanship, ideology, recurring issues, racial attitudes, and economics and politics.[14] As our reviews of these two criteria will illustrate, none of these measures are new to the study of electoral politics, and so we offer a summary account of just how they have been understood as relevant to voter choice, to provide insight into their theoretical importance in the development of the understanding of voter behavior.

Partisanship

Campbell, Gurin, and Miller (1954) launched the theory and measurement of party identification as it is currently understood today, followed shortly thereafter by Campbell et al. in *The American Voter* (1960). Collectively, these researchers developed the concept of party identification and argued for its centrality in understanding American public opinion relevant to voting. Its strengths, they said, were how widespread partisan identities were among the public, how important these were for structuring how the public relates to the political and especially the electoral world, how early they form, and how durable the attachments usually are.

Campbell, Gurin, and Miller used (and the ANES still uses) a two-question battery to measure this concept. The opening question is: "Generally speaking, do you think of yourself as a Republican, a Democrat, an Independent, or what?" Those who said either Republican or Democrat were then asked if they think of themselves "as a strong or a not very strong" party identifier. Those who responded as Independents were asked if they thought of themselves "as closer to the Republican or Democratic Party."

WHAT ARE THEY, AND HOW MANY ARE THERE? 21

The researchers then used these two questions to form a seven-point scale, "Strong Democrat, Weak Democrat, Independent Democrat, Independent, Independent Republican, Weak Republican, and Strong Republican."[15] They called those who said they thought of themselves as Independents but then said they felt closer to a party "Independent Democrats" and "Independent Republicans." It has become conventional since then to call such respondents "leaners," although that is a word not employed in the question, and "leaner" suggests a different interpretation than Independent Democrat or Independent Republican. While the data supported the idea that leaners were less strongly identified with their party than were weak partisans, it has subsequently become clear that leaners often think more like strong than like weak partisans—and act that way (see, e.g., Keith et al. 1992). On the other hand, we also need to respect respondents who said they think of themselves as Independents first, even if they then admitted to feeling closer to one party than the other. Finally, only those with no "leaning" were categorized as truly Independent (aka "pure Independents"), while third-party identifiers and those who could not relate to the questions even to respond meaningfully were given "off scale" scores (the latter, or "apoliticals," varied from 4 to 10 percent of respondents; almost no one identified with a third party).

Over the researchers' seven surveys in the 1950s, "pure Independents" varied from 3 to 8 percent of those scaled (see Campbell et al. 1960, Table 6-1, 124). That is to say, very few respondents did not have some partisan identification, at least if pushed. Campbell and colleagues found that Independent Democrats varied from 6 to 10 percent, while Independent Republicans varied from 4 to 8 percent. That meant that in October 1952, for example, 84 percent were either strong or weak identifiers with a major party, and this varied little over the decade. Thus, most citizens indeed related to one of the two political parties.

The electorate was also more likely to respond with the Democratic Party identifier. In October 1952, 47 percent of respondents were strong or weak Democrats (and 10 percent were Independent Democrats), while 27 percent of the electorate claimed to be strong or weak Republicans and 7 percent were Republican "leaners." That roughly 60–40 Democratic advantage, typical of that decade, provided an interesting challenge to Campbell and colleagues. If partisan identification was so important for understanding public opinion and voting behavior, how could a mostly Democratic-identifying public have elected a Republican president and congressional majority in 1952 and reelected that Republican president by a landslide in 1956? Their answer,

22   THE FUNDAMENTAL VOTER

like ours, is about how to understand the role of this fundamental force in American elections.

Of the several important scholars working on this project, Converse was the major theorist of the concept. The formal mathematics of what he called the "concept of the normal vote" (Converse in Campbell et al. 1966) detailed how partisanship structures voter choice. This structure could be understood as an equilibrium account of what would happen if there were no short-term forces at all (or they just balanced out) or if, in his words, the election took place between a pair of "faceless, nameless, issueless candidates."[16] This notion that party identification could, in effect, be nearly content free was not merely a turn of phrase. Partisanship was understood to develop early in life, well before it could have such political content as that provided by issues, ideology, or anything else, because young children could not respond to such "content-full" ideas about politics.[17] Indeed, it was understood that the earliest identification was most likely transmitted from parent to child, often without conscious attempt by the parents to create any political leanings in the child (e.g., Jennings and Niemi 1968).

Since those pathbreaking works, political scientists have reinvigorated the study of party identification. Currently, many favor a view of partisanship that sees party loyalties as a (or perhaps as *the*) core political identity that many in the public bring to politics (see, e.g., Green et al. 2004; Mason 2018). Indeed, the idea that partisan identification is akin to a "tribal" identity figures prominently even among many leading pundits (see, e.g., Zitner 2023; Woodruff and Carlson 2023). But there is something *more*, and that something is drawing new attention to the importance of party: partisanship's emotional component. Negative affect toward the other party appears to be the major force in the growth of what is known as "affective partisanship" (Iyengar et al. 2019).

We fully agree that there are affective, emotional attributes to partisanship, just as there likely are to ideology and other political orientations, beliefs, preferences, and values (consider the public's reactions to *Roe v. Wade* and to its overturning in *Dobbs v. Jackson Women's Health Organization*), and we agree that these appear to be stronger in recent years than in preceding decades. However, as we will show, the rising coherence and reinforcing nature of the fundamentals, with ideology and issues being a central and increasingly strong part of that coherence, means that alongside surging strong emotional components of partisanship, there is also a growing political substance contributing to what partisanship might mean to the voter.

This pairing should not be a surprise. Emotion and cognition are two of the central components of attitudes and beliefs from a (political) psychology perspective, just as intensity of preference is a key aspect in utility theory, in rational choice theory, and in related accounts of economics and politics, to go along with its otherwise seemingly coldly calculated balancing of costs and benefits.[18] We believe that our evidence adds two important features to the understanding of partisanship. The first is a large dose of the substance of politics in partisanship. We see substantive politics as a complement to and not a substitute for the current emphasis on the importance of identity and emotion in partisanship. Second, our findings help tie together the picture of partisanship presented by scholars in the 1950s, which contained relatively low levels of substantive content and relatively positive evaluations of parties and candidates, with the current understanding of much more strongly negative affective partisanship that is leavened with increasing substance as well, or so we claim. Let's begin developing that claim by considering ideology.

Ideology

Campbell and his colleagues considered carefully the possibility that ideology would stand as a long-term force in place of, or at least in addition to, partisanship.[19] They believed it could serve as a competing long-term force for those for whom ideology was a meaningful concept. We view partisanship and ideology today as complementary rather than competitive. The problem in Campbell and colleagues' view of seeing ideology as a long-term force was that, according to their measurement strategy, very few were able to respond meaningfully to the idea of ideology. They typically found under 10 percent in their samples to be "ideological," with only a slightly greater percentage who were considered "near ideologues."[20] This low level of availability of ideology paled in comparison to the availability of partisanship. So low was the incidence that subsequent scholars often called the electorate "ideologically innocent."

Converse (2006) extended the accounts begun in *The American Voter* in several important ways, including focusing even more than originally done on issues as a potential component of ideology, and it was his work added to that of Campbell et al. (1960) that led others to the conclusion that the public was "innocent" of ideology. If ideology were to be critical in its role as a long-term orienting force, Converse reasoned, it would need to help tie the

24   THE FUNDAMENTAL VOTER

electorate and the political elite together in much the same way that partisanship did. If a citizen held a unique, personal version of ideology (perhaps as discussed in Lane 1962), but could not relate that personal vision to how politicians campaigned on ideology, then ideology would not be serving the role of helping voters make sense of electoral politics. Converse's claim was that the only candidate for such a shared, mass-elite ideology was something similar to a liberal-conservative dimension. He began by noting how the change from Democratic victories to ones won by Republicans in the 1950s was understood:

> And this change in mass voting was frequently interpreted as a shift in public mood from liberal to conservative, a mass desire for a period of respite and consolidation after the rapid liberal innovations of the 1930s and 1940s. Such an account presumes, once again, that [ideologically imposed] constraints visible at an elite level are mirrored in the mass public and that a person choosing to vote Republican after a decade or two of Democratic voting saw himself in some sense or other as giving up a more liberal choice in favor of a more conservative one. (1964, 13)

To Converse, the elites had this understanding of politics in left-right terms, but the electorate, for the most part, did not. Thus, a candidate telling a voter that she is a conservative Republican would provide a basis on which the voter could orient himself toward the candidate and begin to make sense of her candidacy. But if the voter did not understand what "conservative" meant, due to their innocence of ideology, the respondent would only hear and find useful "Republican." That is, for many voters only partisanship served as a long-term force. It was the absence of this specific and critical sense of a shared ideological framework that made the electorate innocent, an innocence that made it harder for a voter to come to grips with electoral politics.

Converse's conclusions launched a very large cottage industry reexamining the evidence, one that continued for decades (for reviews, see Kinder 1983a, updated in Kinder and Kalmoe 2017; see also Achen and Bartels 2016). The surge in partisan polarization and seeming alignment of party with ideology and/or issues led many to expect that this new world would lead to different empirical patterns today than when Converse wrote. Surely the public had lost its innocence over the decades. Kinder and Kalmoe, however, after a close reexamination of much of the empirical data, concluded that the various changes have not been large enough to fundamentally alter Converse's original conclusions. Today, they argue, the electorate remains largely innocent of ideology.

Looking at much of the same data, we reach a different conclusion. We believe that our evidence will show that the glass is (at least) half full rather than half empty. We do not question Kinder and Kalmoe's methods or evidence. We think their evidence, like ours, leads to the conclusion that the electorate should no longer be thought of as (nearly) completely innocent of ideology.[21] Rather, a sufficiently large fraction of the population must now confess to the venal sin of ideological awareness, but not (or not yet, anyway) to the mortal sin of thinking ideologically.

Consider the relationship among party identification, ideology, and a three-policy measure of long-term issue attitudes, the latter two of which began to be asked regularly starting with the 1972 ANES. Party and ideology were correlated at about 0.32 in 1972, when the seven-point ideology measure first appeared. This would be a genuine correlation to be sure, but it would be considered low, especially between a pair of variables thought to be fundamental to understanding politics. The party-ideology correlation, however, increased sharply over time, such that it more than doubled, to over 0.71 in 2020. Similarly, the correlation between issues and partisanship was 0.20 in 1972 and 0.64 in 2020.[22] These are by now sufficiently large correlations with party identification to have moved the assessment from a modest, weak relationship to one sufficiently robust to consider it as "at least half full," or in our thinking, more than half full. Thus, a much larger proportion of the electorate appears to find ideology a meaningful term, and responses to it have become much more closely related both to partisanship and to recurring issues. Ideology now appears to be fundamental.

Recurring Issues

In *The American Voter* (1960), the authors examined closely the question of the role of issues in shaping voter behavior. They proposed what they called the "conditions" for casting a policy-related vote. They found that on average about one in four respondents met these "necessary" conditions for casting such a policy-related vote. And of course they had at hand only policy measures that they considered important enough to ask about in the survey, so

26 THE FUNDAMENTAL VOTER

that 25 percent seemed like a high-water mark. Surely it would be the case that the public would have a lesser ability to vote on less relevant issues.

Yet as we will see in Chapter 3, our data indicate that from 1972 to 2020, the growth in the electorate's ability to vote on issues is remarkable. In the 1970s, as in the 1950s, only about one in four voters tended to meet the *American Voter* criteria, but about *seven in ten* met those criteria in the most recent elections. This is a jump of sufficient magnitude as to consider the glass "well more than half full." This certainly does not mean that voters reason ideologically or through the use of issues, but it does mean that they can and apparently do relate to these scales, at least in some basic way, much as the elites do. To paraphrase Converse, we believe that an electorate that went from voting for a unified Democratic majority in Washington in 2008 to a strong Republican majority in Congress in 2010 was a more conservative voting electorate in 2010 than it was in 2008. Indeed, a majority apparently knew that they were changing their vote from supporting the liberal to supporting the conservative party.[23]

We believe that political issues are not, or not just, matters relevant for the immediate election, as the issues that voting criteria are primarily designed to measure, but also may be of continuing relevance for long periods of time. That is, we believe that issues can serve as a fundamental. Some issues have proven of durable relevance in electoral politics, and we use repeated measurement of the same issue in the same way for decades by the ANES as evidence of this. For example, consider government provision of healthcare. Its contemporary manifestation as the Affordable Care Act, or what is now called by the bipartisan shorthand term "Obamacare," certainly made healthcare a highly contentious issue in 2012 and 2016, but it has also been an issue under various degrees of consideration since the 1950s, with doctors and the American Medical Association helping scuttle government provision of health insurance in those years due to its taint of "creeping socialism." Similarly, Medicare and Medicaid were core elements of Lyndon B. Johnson's Great Society and War on Poverty initiatives in the 1960s. Plans for the government to provide access to healthcare bedeviled the Clinton administration in the 1990s. Thus, whether and how the government should provide healthcare has proven to be a durable question. Issues, that is, can be relevant over the course of many elections, just as they may well be of special relevance in particular elections.

In addition to government healthcare, we consider four other durable policy issues: whether or not the government should play a role in providing jobs and ensuring a good standard of living, whether defense spending should be increased or decreased, whether the government should provide more or fewer services, and whether the government should provide aid to minority groups.[24] Because some of these measures only appeared in current form in the ANES surveys after 1980, our earlier models can tap into only three of the issue areas (health insurance, government provision of jobs, and aid to minority groups), whereas for later years we are able to take advantage of all five.

Campbell et al. (1960) concluded that voters rarely could use policy issues as a basis of either long-term orientations to politics or electoral choice, because too few of them had sufficient information to be able to use the issues for determining their votes. Yet recurring issues increasingly form a strong scale among themselves, and citizens increasingly respond to these scales in terms that meet the "criteria for casting an issue vote" laid out long ago by the authors of *The American Voter* (1960). Even the relatively sparse three-issue scale that extends back to 1972 helps create a measure of issues as a fundamental at levels on a par with party identification and ideology. We will also soon see that the finding that issues are increasingly closely aligned with partisanship and ideology is one of the central indicators of the growing reinforcement among the fundamentals, creating a broad and deep line of electoral cleavage.

Racial Attitudes

It may be so obvious as to need no justification to include racial attitudes as a fundamental force in American politics. Race has been at the center of American politics since the colonial era and was a perplexing issue in the drafting of the Constitution, and its strong relationship to our two current parties dates to the creation of the Republican Party in the 1850s. Emancipation, the Civil War amendments, and Reconstruction brought a biracial Republican Party to power in the South. This coalition was dramatically reversed at the end of Reconstruction. "Redemption," the returning of White southern Democrats to power and the Jim Crow system they subsequently imposed, both suppressed Black political rights in the South and created the one-party system of the "lily white" Democratic Party, containing virtually all meaningful political competition within it. Jim Crow reversed the gains of the Civil War and Reconstruction and effectively eliminated the

28 THE FUNDAMENTAL VOTER

Republican Party (and all others that might conceivably have opposed the Democrats) as an organized entity in the South for three-quarters of a century.[25] This not only affected African American political attitudes and even the attitudes of White southerners, but also shaped the policy views of the national electorate. Miller and Stokes (1963) showed that clusters of seemingly closely related issues were often weakly related among the public in their consideration of congressional representation of public policy beliefs. The dramatic exception was the set of civil rights issue questions they studied (as it was in Converse 2006). They found that the congressional representative understood (accurately enough) where the district stood on race, with a paired correlation three times larger than that of other issue clusters (Miller and Stokes 1963, 52).

That new system was durable in the South. The remnants of Jim Crow were still being dismantled in 1972, when our principal time series begins. Indeed, perhaps the most important national figure of the White supremacist southern Democrats at that time, Governor George C. Wallace (AL), ran for the Democratic nomination for president in 1972, before being seriously wounded in an assassination attempt while campaigning. This end to his leadership of the segregationist South coincided with a change in political discourse in the country. It became understood that one could no longer use crude racist language in public, as Wallace had, but instead had to shift to a more carefully coded language, cloaking plausibly racist campaign themes in less virulent language. It remains unclear, and a point of some debate, whether true beliefs also changed at the time.

In either case, just how to measure racial attitudes in the electorate had to change as well. Instead of direct use of terms such as *lazy, stupid*, or *criminal*, or similarly worded (or worse) dehumanizing themes (Jardina and Piston 2023; Kteily and Bruneau 2017), the "new racism" had to be measured by phrases such as "affirmative action," "unfair advantages," and "reverse discrimination." Indeed, one of the important lessons of the infamous Willie Horton ad (run by the senior Bush campaign in 1988) was that direct use of the earlier, overtly racist language raised awareness of and defenses against responding to it in ways to make respondents appear racist (see, notably, Mendelberg 2001). Only when coded in the language of this "new" racism would a substantial portion of the public reject policies designed to ameliorate the plight of racial minorities. Recognizing this, scholars developed a new measure for tapping into racial attitudes. The scale we use was originally called "modern racism" (McConahay 1983) and then "symbolic racism"

(Sears 1988), then changed titles once again to become what is now known as the "racial resentment" scale.[26]

Most minorities, of course, but especially African Americans, report Democratic identification; of those who do not, nearly all claim to be Independents. Black citizens began to move away from Republican loyalties as the party of Lincoln and emancipation and toward Democratic identification during Roosevelt's New Deal (especially around 1936). In the 1960s the civil rights movement; Goldwater's vote against the Civil Rights Act in 1964 (just as he was becoming Republican presidential nominee); and President Lyndon Johnson's championing of the Civil Rights and Voting Rights Acts, along with his Great Society and War on Poverty programs, turned Black Americans toward the Democratic Party. Figures 2.1 and 2.2 show just how quickly Black partisanship changed in the mid-1960s in light of the events of that period.

The first figure shows the percentages of Blacks and White respondents who were coded as "apolitical" in response to the party identification questions.[27] The change in that figure is dramatic. Among White respondents, very few

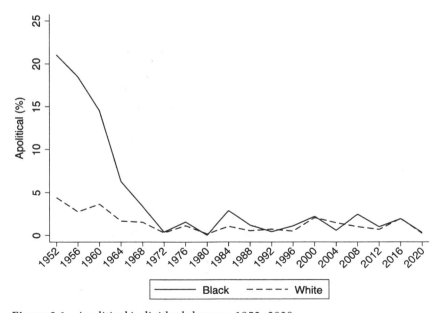

Figure 2.1. Apolitical individuals by race, 1952–2020

Source: Compiled by authors from the ANES Time Series Cumulative Study, the 2000 ANES Time Series Study, and the 2016 ANES Time Series Study.

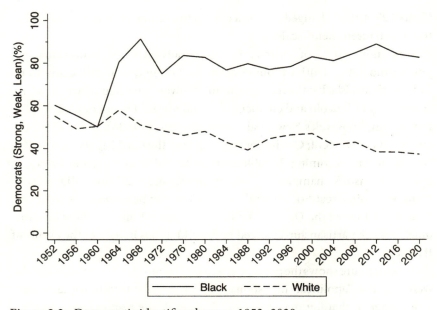

Figure 2.2. Democratic identifiers by race, 1952–2020
Source: Compiled by authors from the ANES Time Series Cumulative Study, the 2000 ANES Time Series Study, and the 2016 ANES Time Series Study.

ever identified as "apolitical," typically no more than 1 to 4 percent. Among Black respondents the percentage was 15 percent or more—until the civil rights movement, the March on Washington in 1963, the Civil Rights Act in 1964, and the Voting Rights Act in 1965. When politics could imaginably include African Americans and could lead to policies positively supporting their rights as citizens, the percentages of African Americans responding as "apolitical" plunged at once to percentages very similar to those among White respondents.

It was immediately clear to African Americans that Johnson and the Democratic Party were acting to include them, while Goldwater and the Republicans were opposing them.[28] Through 1960, Black and White citizens differed little in their partisanship, as Figure 2.2 shows, but starting in 1962, African American partisan identification jumped from the approximately 50 percent it had been in the Eisenhower era to the 80 percent, and even more, it reached from 1964 on. As with "apoliticals," White identification with the Democratic Party changed little and slowly, hovering at or above 50 percent from 1952 through about 1980, slowly declining to about

37 percent in 2020.[29] The very rapid changes in partisanship among African Americans illustrate the speed with which partisan identification can change in response to dramatic changes in social and political circumstances.

It is also the case that the idea of identity is truly central to the way social scientists study and think about racial and ethnic politics. Especially for African Americans, it is their identity as African Americans, rather than their partisan identity, that matters (see Dawson 1995; Tate 1994).Or perhaps it is their racial and ethnic identity—and the substantive politics and policy of the two parties—that has shaped (and perhaps caused) any partisan identity they may have. They are oriented toward the political system less by "tribal" and content-free, affective evaluations of political parties and more by race and the substantive actions of the two parties.

Spearheaded by Dawson through his "black utility heuristic" and resulting "linked fate" (the belief that what is good for fellow Black people is good for the individual Black person; see Dawson 1995), African American voting patterns move to a different dynamic than Whites'. Dawson's account became even more clearly understood as the idea of social identity came to prominence in the social and behavioral sciences (Tajfel 1996; Tajfel and Turner 1978; Tajfel et al. 1979; Huddy 2001). It seems clear that while many African Americans might have a partisan identity, it is their racial identity that shapes their political beliefs and thereby their partisan identity. And in that identity's translation to politics (Huddy 2001), it seems equally clear that there is not only a strong affective, emotive base to it, but also a very strong substance base in politics and policy, as Figures 2.1 and 2.2 illustrate.

It is still a matter of some uncertainty how well this conclusion—racial identity being the dominant force for understanding orientation toward electoral politics—holds for other racial and ethnic identities (McClain et al. 2009). It is at least the case that Latino and other racial and ethnic minorities have social identities that are different from being a simple manifestation of their political identity as a partisan. Moreover, it is impossible to make sense of their electoral choices without understanding the direct and substantial effects of the actions and policies of the two parties in shaping their political orientations.

We thus conclude that the politics of racial and ethnic minorities is based on some as yet uncertain mixture of their social identity, their political and partisan identity, and the politics and policies of the parties between which they choose. As important as the development of partisan identity as a political identity is, and as important and substantial as the growth in affective

32 THE FUNDAMENTAL VOTER

evaluations in partisanship may be, partisanship clearly is not at the center of politics, by itself and alone. Indeed, for the nearly 40 percent of the adult public who are racial or ethnic minorities, partisanship appears pretty clearly not to be the unique and central feature that forms their exclusive orientation to politics. Their racial and ethnic identities are perhaps paramount and thus also the bases on which these identities align with electoral politics, and thus they align the triumvirate of issues, ideology, and partisanship.

For the remaining White majority, partisanship is of course very important and probably more so as a social identity than is their race. Perhaps, as Jardina (2019) argues, Whites have a social identity as a racial group that, like those of racial and ethnic minorities, is at least one ingredient for understanding their politics in contemporary America. Indeed, some argue that the fear of becoming a minority in America underlies at least some of the "turn" to White identity.

Economics and Politics

The influence of the economy is likely the oldest and most established set of empirical findings on elections (e.g., Tibbitts 1931; Ogburn and Hill 1935). There has been considerable controversy over just how that relationship might play out in electoral dynamics. Many assume a version of what is referred to by economists as "narrow self-interest"; that is, voters respond to how the economy affects their own circumstances and engage in "pocketbook voting." Indeed, politicians and media often imagine that a tax cut will generate votes by putting more money in voters' wallets, thereby making the public grateful for the extra cash.

Others argue that it is not how the political economy affects voters *individually* that matters, but how the economy *overall* is doing that has the larger effect on society and thus shapes voter decisions. Thus, for example, a tax cut might stimulate economic growth, and as a result the country is made better off. Voters will then reward those policymakers who put forth the tax cut. Even here, however, there has been controversy. What part(s) of the economy matter(s)? Is it, as in the last example, economic growth, or might it be changes in (real, disposable) income that matters, or rising unemployment, or the rate of inflation?

A first approach is to ask if the public perceives how well the current political leaders in Washington are doing in managing the economy. Bad management, in this view, is related to voting against the incumbents, while good circumstances might lead voters to reward them (e.g., Tufte 1978). Others argue that there is a partisan division in terms of the political economy (e.g., Hibbs and Hibbs 1989). Democrats are the party that has historically attended more to unemployment, while Republicans have been the party that has worked harder to mitigate inflation. Perhaps surprisingly, this partisan differentiation on what parts of the economy most affect their voting base has become less important to party elites, in spite of increasing partisan polarization (e.g., Duch and Stevenson 2008). Further, this is so even though overall economic performance is now taken as one of the central concerns of voters, or at least it is no less important than during the less polarized era. In addition, it has come to be understood that voters respond more, in the aggregate, to national conditions rather than voting their pocketbook. Indeed, predictions of election outcomes are often centered on the state of the national economy more than any other explanation.

One might think that absent concern over just precisely which measure of the state of the economy to use, agreement that the economy is important and how the incumbents have handled the economy is what matters most would have ended most of the controversy. These are the days of partisan polarization, however. So even here, partisan differences might be expected to arise, and not so much (at least in current thinking) in terms of whether unemployment is a Democratic issue and inflation a Republican one. Instead, the concern is that people disagree with those in the opposing party over *everything*, including such seemingly evident facts as the actual, factual conditions of the American economy. How could that be so?

Motivated reasoning is a fast-growing topic of research in political psychology (Lodge and Taber 2013; Taber and Lodge 2006; see more recently Bolsen and Palm 2019; Tappin, Pennycock, and Rand 2020). Motivated reasoning includes, in part, rationalization. This has a long history in psychology. We might start with Leon Festinger, who developed the notion of cognitive dissonance in the 1950s (Festinger 1962; Greenwald and Ronis 1978). He argued that humans desire to strike a balance in valances (i.e., positive or negative affect) among the evaluations of, let us say, a presidential candidate, her position on an issue, and the voter's own attitude on that issue. He might like the candidate, favor greater spending for healthcare, and then hear that she is opposed to increased spending on healthcare. Her position is out of balance with his, then, and creates dissonance in his thinking. To put it back into balance, the voter might change his position on the issue,

34 THE FUNDAMENTAL VOTER

thereby coming to be (or appear to be) convinced by that favored candidate. Or he might decide to no longer support that candidate. Or perhaps he will decide that this issue really isn't important and look instead at other issues or concerns for supporting the favored candidate.

There is one more option in this set. A voter simply might not *believe* the candidate really opposes increased support for healthcare, perhaps despite the evidence. This denial of what those outside one's dissonant system might perceive as obvious facts is what is generating the most discussion these days, perhaps because it is the most important dissonance reduction technique in national politics today. Many conservatives deny the existence of climate change, even though it appears to be here, now. Many liberals deny that the benefits of vaccinations vastly outweigh the tiny costs, with increasing deaths from measles and other preventable diseases happening in contemporary America.[30] Of course the COVID-19 pandemic has changed vaccine politics, so that it is conservative Republicans who are the principal (but not exclusive) vaccine deniers now.

It is certainly correct that "fake news" and believing in people, processes, or policies against all evidence are now common and perhaps increasingly so. If these tendencies are growing in prevalence, it might well be a consequence of the increasing reinforcement of cleavages. It was one thing when many, but not all, Democrats (Republicans) were on one side on some issues and on the other side on other issues. Policy consistency was not particularly at issue for political elites in the era of crosscutting cleavages, so why should such consistency be expected to be found among voters? The consequence of being out of sync, when most everyone else was also from time to time, generated relatively small amounts of dissonance. But now that Republicans are (almost) always on one side, and Democrats are (almost) always on the other, dissonance is more than an occasional nuisance.[31] Facts one hears as being alleged all of a sudden take on heightened importance. One useful strategy is to deny the truth value of the facts, especially when Republican elites are telling a voter that there is no climate change, and similarly for Democratic activists telling their tall tales about vaccines. And of course if politicians and media are both seen as ordinarily taking sides, then a voter has little recourse to judge the truth value of at least some claims of fact.

In the 1970s and 1980s, the psychologists Daniel Kahneman (eventual Nobel laureate in economics) and Amos Tversky (who surely would also have been so, except for his untimely death) cataloged the use of various "biases and heuristics" in decision-making (Tversky and Kahneman 1986;

Kahneman, Slovic, and Tversky 1982).[32] They used the conventional economic account of "rationality," the standard model for explaining consumer behavior and economic outcomes generally, as the basis for assessing biases. Each bias and each heuristic moved the individual to the use of information in ways that had the potential to deflect them from their "rational" choice, by which the researchers meant the optimal choice for the individual based on the truth.

At about the same time, there was a growing branch of political science that applied economic-style rational choice to political choosing, with considerable attention paid to the way economic conditions shaped political behavior. While there were contradictory findings, overall, elections appeared to move with the economy in predictable ways. Over time, the accumulation of evidence from around the democratic world has led to an all but undeniable conclusion: economic conditions are a consequential force in shaping political outcomes (Duch and Stevenson 2006, 2010; Lewis-Beck 1990; Lewis-Beck and Stegmaier 2000; Powell and Whitten 1993).

As we noted earlier, the evidence was reasonably clear that voters do not very often "vote their pocketbook," but they do reward politicians who are incumbents during times when there is a strong economy and punish those who are not. Citizens, it appears, respond to national economic conditions but not to personal economic circumstances. There is an obvious explanation for why economic voting is difficult to find at the individual level. By and large, there is but one national economy, and it is growing, doing well, shrinking, or doing poorly for most of its citizens, although rarely for all of them at the same time. The condition of the national economy is a fact, and what we are measuring is opinions that vary about an essentially fixed fact about the economy.

Consider Kramer's (1983) work concerning the importance of the economy in congressional elections over the twentieth century. As he pointed out, he used variation in the real economy over that time to explain changes in voting for Congress.[33] That is, he was looking at electoral choices over time in comparison to changes in the actual economy, and it was those changes themselves, not perceptions of economic fortunes, let alone rationalizations or motivated reasons, that appeared to shape voter behavior. Those who disparaged the voter via survey evidence were, he argued, generally looking at the effect of measurement error—that is, those who mistakenly thought the economy was doing great when it was not and those who erroneously thought it was doing awfully even when it was doing well. Erikson, MacKuen,

36   THE FUNDAMENTAL VOTER

and Stimson (1998, 2002) provided some firmer estimates via their mixture of over-time and cross-sectional data.

Achen and Bartels (2016; but see Fowler and Hall 2018) in effect mocked the American voter by pointing out that Democrats in New Jersey who lived near the ocean turned against Woodrow Wilson for president in 1916 apparently in light of a series of shark attacks (those that eventually gave rise to the script for the movie *Jaws*). They used that narrative in part to critique one of the most important kinds of economic voting, "retrospective voting." There are various forms of this concept, attributable to Key and to Downs and Fiorina,[34] but the basic point is that citizens are more likely to support incumbents who have presided over good economic circumstances and less likely to do so when incumbents have presided over poor economic circumstances.[35] This can work, but only if voters actually perceive whether they have just experienced good or bad times.[36] If incumbent parties and their leaders could convince their partisans that times were good even when they were bad, and out-party elites could convince their partisans that times were bad even when they were good, then any connection between reports of economic conditions and the vote would be specious.

Of course, except at the margin, it is rare that one could imaginably convince a voter that times were good when they actually were bad (did people not notice that they were living in the midst of the Great Depression?), and vice versa. The margin is much more modest than that. Indeed, Achen and Bartels (2016) pointed out (as we do below) that the public does respond to changes in the true economy. Their point was that, in their estimation, holding incumbents responsible for all sorts of conditions, including the economy, is not a very good method for holding democratically elected leaders accountable. This was the reason they developed the "shark attack" example, for instance. They could thereby credibly argue that it appears that leaders were being held accountable for events and circumstances over which they had little control.

Some argue, quite plausibly, that presidents actually have very little control over the economy.[37] Perhaps this explains why Trump (and other presidents before him) leaned hard on the Federal Reserve Board, which does play a significant role in shaping economic conditions, to reflect presidential preferences in their actions. More importantly, of course, Trump and now Joseph R. "Joe" Biden, Jr. follow every other modern president in working hard to take credit for good economic conditions and to deflect responsibility for bad ones. That the president says he is responsible makes it plausible that voters would thereby hold him accountable. Or as Aldrich et al.

(2014) demonstrate for Obama, voters did not blame Barack Obama and the Democrats for causing the "Great Recession" of 2007–2008, but they did blame them for not fixing those conditions more rapidly. So the evidence is that there is a bit of nuance to the way citizens hold their government accountable for economic conditions.

To conclude, while there certainly is rationalization, indeed sometimes truly substantial amounts of it, along with party-leadership-centered campaigns that achieve some successful level of motivated reasoning, it is worth reflecting on Kramer's (1983) central message. In particular, if public opinion includes a healthy dose of responsiveness to real-world conditions, then there is some room for retrospective voting. It is not all dissonance reduction, cognitive balancing, and motivated reasoning. And that is the role that economic retrospection plays in our account of the set of fundamentals. Our evidence is quite strong for over-time movement of average perceptions among the public as a whole compared to the actual economic circumstances, as the data in Figure 2.3 document.[38] When times were good, the average

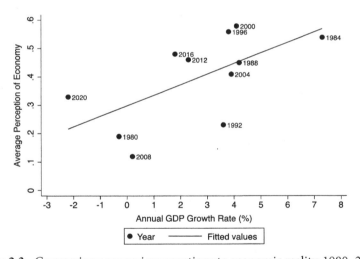

Figure 2.3. Comparing economic perceptions to economic reality, 1980–2020

Note: Line shows the linear fit prediction between the economic perception and economic reality. Average perception of economy represents mean values of the retrospective economic evaluation variable, where higher values indicate positive evaluations that the national economy has "gotten better" in the preceding year. Annual GDP growth rate data reflect the average of quarterly real gross domestic product percent changes from the previous year.

Source: Compiled by authors from the ANES Time Series Cumulative Data File, the 2000 ANES Time Series Study, and the 2016 ANES Time Series Study. GDP growth rate data from the US Bureau of Economic Analysis, retrieved from the Federal Reserve Bank of St. Louis, https://fred.stlouisfed.org/series/A191RO1Q156NBEA.

voter agreed that times had been good. When times were bad, the public, as a whole, agreed that times had been bad. This is another instance of "half full" in a literature that focuses on the glass being entirely empty.

Conclusion

We have now outlined some of the theories that social scientists have developed for understanding electoral behavior, and we have indicated how we believe you should understand them, noting how our view is often different from those of others. Putting the pieces together, however, indicates how deeply important social scientists believe each of these factors is in shaping public opinion and electoral choice. Whether you agree with our initial theorizing about each component, we hope you understand that these are indeed fundamental forces. That is, so far we have made a case for three of the four criteria for each of these being a fundamental force in electoral politics.

In summary, we have shown that each of these candidates for electoral fundamental forces have been an enduring feature of American electoral politics as, for example, the dates of the citations illustrate. Each therefore arouses claims and debates about consequential theoretical meaning and empirical potency. Moreover, these are not theories of "how Biden won" or other unique and time-specific explanations of electoral outcomes. They are not accounts dependent upon candidates or campaigns "mattering," although surely they do, but rather are accounts dependent upon whether, how, and why partisan identification, ideology, issues, race, and the economy matter in voters' understanding of politics and guiding their decision-making. Our tentative answer at this point—to why Campbell and colleagues, based on data from the 1950s, concluded that partisanship was the sole fundamental force guiding most citizens and why we are claiming that several more are by now relevant—is the low incidence of apparent meaning and utilization of issues, ideology, and so on at that time and the growth in their meaning and relevance in the electorate today. We have also given some evidence that suggests that these fundamentals are strongly connected to how and why citizens vote as they do, but it is time to assess more fully and carefully the empirical bases for these connections and how they have changed over time.

3

The Fundamentals and the Vote, 1952–2020

Republican Ronald Reagan easily won the presidency in 1980, and the Republicans won a majority in the Senate that year for the first time in a quarter century. In the House, even though the Democrats lost 34 seats, they retained their majority, holding a comfortable 243 to 192 lead. One of the most important issues in that Congress was the budget for the coming 1982 fiscal year. The budget is obviously an important piece of legislation in any Congress, but it was especially so that year, having been a centerpiece of Reagan's and many congressional Republicans' campaigns. The Constitution requires that spending bills originate in the House. The Democrats put forward the majority party's plan, which usually is the central focus of debate and almost invariably passes the House, even if amended heavily. That plan, however, was defeated on the floor when twenty-nine mostly southern conservative Democrats defected to support proposals advanced by the opposition party's president. Such a large number of defections from the majority party on such a critical part of the agenda is virtually unthinkable today.[1] Even the most moderate majority party members, who may think their own party is pushing too far toward the extreme and may not be willing to support such moves, are invariably closer to the typical views of their own party than to those of the opposition. As a result, they may on rare occasions vote to scuttle their own party's plans, but they will not advance plans and programs of their opposition.

The electorate was not as divided in 1980 as it is today, and the event just described was one of the many steps leading to the electoral form of partisan polarization that we will discuss in the next chapter. Electoral polarization does not feature dramatic growth of extremism in the public, as it appears to do in Congress, but its electoral form, or "sorting," does mean that much of the partisan public no longer agrees with the opposition on nearly anything, and as we saw in Chapter 1, partisans today rarely defect to vote against their party's candidates. Much of the driving force behind the electoral version of

The Fundamental Voter. John H. Aldrich, Suhyen Bae, and Bailey K. Sanders, Oxford University Press.
© Oxford University Press 2024. DOI: 10.1093/oso/9780197745489.003.0003

40   THE FUNDAMENTAL VOTER

partisan polarization can be traced to growth in the number of fundamental forces in the way originally identified by Campbell et al. (1960), which will provide the basis for understanding the electoral changes that have occurred since that 1980 contest.

In this chapter we will provide additional evidence beyond that described in Chapter 2 that there are a growing number of fundamental forces orienting citizens to electoral politics, and this growth is primarily due to the increasing number of citizens for whom ideology, durable issues, racial orientations, and economic retrospection are added to partisanship as relevant forces in their political environment. We will also make the case that this enlarged set of fundamentals is increasingly closely related to the vote. Finally, these empirical findings will help us understand the basis for the changes in voting and elections begun in the 1980s. A primary task is to develop the first part of the answer to the questions posed in Chapter 1. This chapter will also set the stage for showing that the electoral polarization is best understood as growth in "sorting" between the partisans over these fundamental forces, and that this has not reduced but enhanced and enriched the role of partisanship in elections. We then turn to consider how this increasingly strong reinforcement of the partisan cleavage has worrying consequences for the state of American democracy.

Why Are There More Fundamentals in the 2020s Than in the 1950s?

As we noted in the last chapter, Campbell et al. (1960) and Converse (2006) justified their claim that partisanship was the single long-term attitude of any importance for orienting voters to politics. It was the important one among those they studied due to the nearly complete absence of any meaningful sense of ideology found among the public and any real ability of citizens to understand issues sufficiently to be able to cast a vote along issue lines. If the public could not use issues to help form voting choices, then even enduring issues could not be in any sense fundamental. In other words, both issues and ideology were failing in the central role of a fundamental, which is to help orient the public to electoral politics.

Note that one consequence of partisanship being the sole long-term attitude for orienting citizens to electoral politics was that partisanship itself, therefore, could not have had much political content. This was so not only because there was not much content to people's political views overall, but also because partisanship was largely unrelated to ideology, issues, race, and economic retrospection among those who did have such considerations available.[2] That left group affiliations for including any political content to partisanship, such as unions being for Democrats, but not much more.[3] There was no ideology or policy or much else to serve as a basis for rendering partisan opinions. Even for the small fraction of the public for whom ideology might be relevant, the fact that partisanship was shown to have formed for many well before reaching voting age was understood as meaning that it was formed long before ideology, issues, or whatever else of substance was available to the citizen to provide political content to partisanship.

Consider what Campbell and colleagues found about ideology in the electorate in the 1950s. Their analysis concluded that only 2.5 percent of respondents (3.5 percent of reported voters) had any meaningful sense of ideology.[4] Another 9 percent (12 percent of voters) were classified as "near ideologues," which they defined as "including persons who used one or more of the labels common to ideological discussion, but in a context rather bare of supporting perceptions" (Campbell et al. 1960, 231). As noted in Chapter 2, this level of utilization contrasts vividly with the eight or even nine in ten for whom partisanship was present and apparently meaningful to the respondent.[5] The difference was so vast, and the number of actual ideologues in their rendering so low, that their conclusion that party identification was a candidate for a long-term force but that ideology was not a serious candidate seemed unquestionable.

ANES data since then provide us with a different way to measure ideology, one that we can apply over time starting in 1972, when the seven-point format was first introduced. We do not know what their reading of these more recent measurements of ideology would have led them to conclude, had the questions been asked in the 1950s.[6] We can, however, trace the evidence at hand from 1972 through 2020, documenting that there was a very large increase in the capability of the electorate to respond meaningfully to ideology as measured by a seven-point scale. The increase is, in our judgment, sufficiently large to permit us to conclude that ideology can now be a plausible candidate for a fundamental force in electoral politics, to go along with partisanship in this category.

Now consider issues (which the researchers folded into ideology). Campbell et al. (1960) argued that most voters did not have a sufficient basis for reasoning about, let alone voting on, the basis of issues. As we noted

42   THE FUNDAMENTAL VOTER

earlier, Campbell et al. (1960) and Converse (2006, 1970) used the absence of issue voting capabilities as part of their explanation of why the voter was typically not an ideologue. Whether issues and ideology are necessarily tied together is a matter of some dispute in the literature (which was Conover and Feldman's [1981] point). Therefore, we consider long-term recurring issues as a third possible long-term attitude to be studied on its own, even if it could or should be considered closely related to ideology and even to partisanship. Indeed, we will study those relationships later on.

Consider, for example, how Campbell and colleagues came to conclude that few voters could vote on the basis of issues. They proposed that a voter could rest her choice of candidate on the basis of an issue only if she was aware of the issue in some form, saw what the candidates or parties offered on that issue, and perceived a difference between the offerings of the two parties or candidates. These, the researchers claimed, were necessary conditions for an issue to matter to a voter's choice, but they were not sufficient ones. Just because they could vote on the basis of an issue (or on the basis of ideology, or of partisanship) does not mean that they did. But if these conditions were not satisfied, then the voter could *not* have voted on the basis of that issue. And the researchers found that about 28 percent of the public could cast a vote on the typical issue included in the survey.[7] As they concluded, "At this level, then, we are forced to conclude that articulation between party program, party member opinion, and individual political opinion is weak, indeed" (Campbell et al. 1960, 187).

Today, however, there is evidence that now there is greater potential for issue voting and, given long-term repeated use of the same issue questions, greater potential for an issue-based fundamental. Abramson et al. (beginning with [1983] and continuing through Aldrich et al. [2022]) have tested these conditions on the seven-point issue scales that we employ in our policy fundamental.[8] They added a fourth criterion, that the voter should also know at least to a very rough approximation where the candidates stand on the issue, which they defined as putting the two candidates in the "correct" order (that is, placing the Democrat to the left of the Republican candidate).[9] They have reported the proportion of the respondents who satisfied all four of these criteria on each issue and averaged them over the various such issues that the ANES included in its survey.[10] We also use the same criteria for assessing the potential usefulness of the seven-point ideology scale with respondents to these surveys from 1972 to 2020. The claim is that if a large enough proportion of the electorate is able to satisfy these criteria for casting an issue-based or an ideology-based vote, and if the issue scale, like the ideology scale, is felt to be sufficiently relevant for inclusion in the ANES surveys over many years, then durable issues, like ideology, are a candidate for a fundamental force in orienting the public to democracy.

The evidence from Abramson and colleagues that supports these claims can be found in Figure 3.1.[11] Note that applying these criteria to ideology is very different from the analysis that Campbell et al. (1960; see also Converse 1969) did with ideology in order to conclude that the electorate was (as it later came to be called) "ideologically innocent." These criteria are more directly measuring ideological responses than in the earlier works.[12] Conversely, while more directly relevant, they also impose less of a burden on the respondent than did Campbell and colleague's measures and thus yield an easier "test" of ideological understanding to "pass."[13] But most importantly for our purposes here, these criteria are regularly available. The proportion who satisfied all four criteria on these two fundamentals, then, are reported in Figure 3.1.

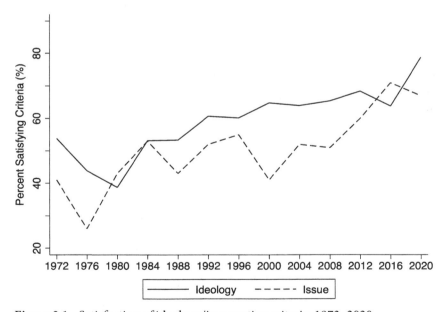

Figure 3.1. Satisfaction of ideology/issue voting criteria, 1972–2020

Source: Data and measure for Ideology criteria compiled by authors from the ANES Time Series Cumulative Study, the 2000 ANES Time Series Study, and the 2016 ANES Time Series Study. Data and measure for Issue voting criteria from Abramson et al. and Aldrich et al., Change and Continuity series, various years.

44 THE FUNDAMENTAL VOTER

In 1972 and 1976, at the start of the survey series, around four in ten respondents satisfied these four criteria on the ideology scale. We cannot, of course, draw a line back to 1952 and 1956, nor could we match up the proportions, due to the different measurement of ideology used back then. Nonetheless, the big story is not the particular levels in any given year; it is the change from as low as 40 percent in 1980 to nearly 80 percent in 2020, an increase that seems sufficiently large as to change the researchers' original conclusion. Whether or not satisfying these criteria means that someone is (or is not) innocent of ideological thinking, the difference from the 1970s to the current time is sharp.

The issue voting scales represent a more direct comparison to the 1950s, since the same criteria were used, although the format of the issue questions was different. We see that only a little more than one in four meet all of the criteria in 1976, even with the addition of the new "correct ordering" criterion, a finding that is not all that different from what was reported for the 1950s. To be sure, 1976 was unique among our recent presidential elections in terms of how similar the two candidates were in fact and were perceived to be by the electorate.[14] Perhaps 1972 or 1980 was more indicative of a "standard" presidential campaign of that era, in which about two in five respondents satisfied all four criteria on the average issue scale. By 2020, that numbers also had increased, quite like the case with the ideology scale, such that on the average issue, two in three satisfied all four criteria. Since respondents are often asked about seven or more issues in that format in each ANES, that means the average respondent could have voted on the basis of five issues. The change is stark and dramatic.[15] It suggests a much more substantive interpretation of the fundamentals. This may be especially important for partisanship, because if party identification, ideology, and issues (and perhaps race and economic considerations) all together help orient the citizen to elections and politics, then there is a lot more substance about politics brought to bear on the short-term attitudes in any given election, and thus also brought to bear on the vote, now than a half century ago.

The American Voter Model, 1956–1976

We cannot directly tie most of our findings onward from 1972 back to the 1950s and the 1960s. Still, there is reason to believe that there was an important evolution in that era. Fortunately, we are able to provide some fairly direct evidence from others to buttress that claim.

The 1960s differed substantially from the 1950s. The 1956 survey provided the central empirical evidence that Campbell and colleagues employed on this question. By that election, the issues that were prominent in 1952 had become less so. Fighting had been suspended in Korea, the McCarthy-era threat to civil liberties and democracy had ended, and the nation was economically buoyant. But the "Happy Days" view of 1956 soon changed even more sharply. The 1960s were more politically contested. The civil rights movement was peaking in its contestation against Jim Crow and racial injustice; the Vietnam War drove a growing number of protests across the nation and generated testy generational and class divides. By the end of the decade, the economy was teetering, inflation was growing, and the state of the economy was declining toward the "stagflation" (the combination of high unemployment and high inflation) of the 1970s. One might well wonder whether the 1950s combination of low issue competence, ideological innocence, and high partisanship was changing, perhaps in ways that would be revealed in the 1960s and 1970s, even with data similar to those used by Campbell and colleagues.

Although we cannot make a clear empirical case for the growth of relevance and importance of long-term forces in the electorate due to the changing nature of the measures, we *can* get a sense of the transition from the 1950s to the 1970s. Several scholars during that time estimated versions of the "funnel of causality" specification through models similar to that presented in Figure 3.2. Most were tested on a specific election, obviating their use for our purposes here. Fortunately, Hartwig et al. (1980) have provided estimates

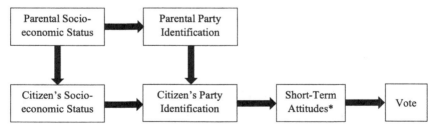

Figure 3.2. Illustrating *The American Voter*'s theory of voting

Note: *Denotes the six short-term attitudes toward the two candidates, domestic and foreign issues, and groups and parties as managers of government.

Source: Compiled by authors based on Campbell et al., *The American Voter* (New York: Wiley, 1960).

of a model similar to that in Figure 3.2 that does provide as close as we can come to a "bridging" analysis for our purposes. While it does not provide that direct test of potentially changing long-term forces, it does provide a systematic look at partisanship and short-term forces, indicating the potential for an increased role for ideology and (long-term) issue preferences in the 1960s and into the 1970s.

We report their results in Figure 3.3, looking at the total effects of party identification, issues, and evaluations of the candidates as a percentage of all three combined.[16] The declining effect of party identification on the vote (relative to how candidate evaluations and issues are also related to the vote) is starkly apparent in their data. Indeed, it is a rather smooth decline, with candidate evaluations all but staying constant and therefore issues picking up influence as the direct relevance of partisanship slumps. Party retains its leading role, but the margin shrinks noticeably, more or less in line with what was anticipated, with a more issue-filled electorate due to a more issue-filled polity. Indeed, a reasonable assessment is that by the 1970s, parties, issues, and candidates are in fair balance, in place of a party-dominated election in 1956. We can examine what has transpired from 1972 through 2020 in more precise and theoretically relevant ways, the topic to which we now turn.

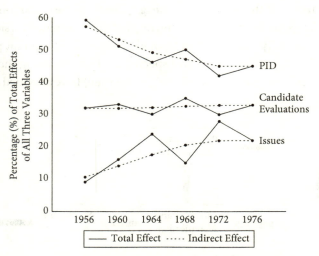

Figure 3.3. Changing role of partisanship, issues, and candidates, 1956–1976
Source: Frederick Hartwig, William R. Jenkins, and Earl M. Temchin, "Variability in Electoral Behavior: The 1960, 1968, and 1976 Elections," *American Journal of Political Science* 24, no. 3 (1980): 555, fig. 1.

How Important Are the Fundamentals in Voting Decisions?

One of our central claims is that the role of fundamental forces in orienting citizens to electoral politics has both broadened and deepened, and we have offered a variety of evidence about this. The last and perhaps the most important evidence is that these electoral forces do appear to help guide voters to their choices in the voting booth. We demonstrate this in this section by showing that the various fundamentals are individually related to the presidential and the congressional votes. We provide two ways of assessing their importance in the vote. One is the simple, direct relationship between the fundamental and the vote. In statistical parlance, this is sometimes called the "full" or "total effect" estimate. This means that it includes not only any direct effect on how people decide ("I like the candidate because she is a Republican") but also any indirect, or "mediated," effects. In the simple "funnel of causality" model in Figure 3.2, all effects of party identification are indirect, mediated through its effect on intervening variables, what Campbell and colleagues refer to as "short-term attitudes." While as far as we can tell, they believed that party identification had no direct effect on the vote, by taking short-term attitudes into account, most who estimated this or similar models (as in Hartwig, Jenkins, and Temchin [1980] in Figure 3.3) allow for a direct effect of partisanship on the vote, as well as its variety of indirect effects. We do that here as well, for all five fundamentals under consideration. As a result, we report two effects. One is the pair-wise correlation of the fundamental and the vote, which gives us our best estimate of the total effect. The second is the partial effect of the fundamental after including ("controlling for") all variables we put into the voting account.[17] This result gives us the best estimate of the direct effect of the fundamental on the vote after controlling for all else.

Our question for now is how strongly and consistently the fundamentals are related to the vote. We answer this visually in Figure 3.4 for the presidential vote and in Figure 3.5 for the congressional vote.[18] There are five panels in each figure, one for assessing the relationship of each of the fundamentals to the vote. We draw two lines in each case. The solid line is the "first difference" in predicted probability of voting from the full model reported above, that is, including all fundamentals and the socioeconomic status (SES) variables.[19] This is an estimate of the direct effect. The dotted line is the same kind of first difference, except that it is from the bivariate relationship between that

48   THE FUNDAMENTAL VOTER

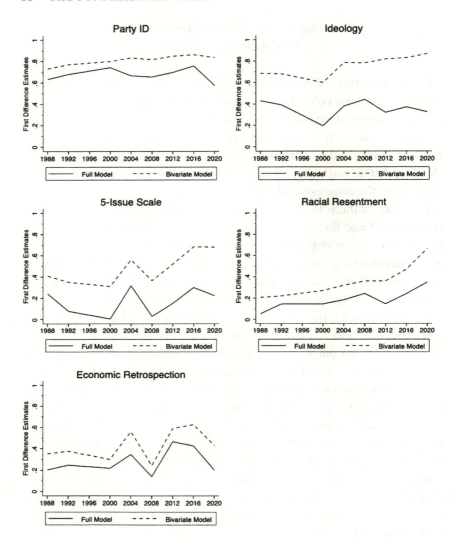

Figure 3.4. Fundamentals and their effect on presidential vote, 1988–2020

Note: Estimates derived by calculating the difference of predicted probabilities at the 25th and 75th percentile values of each fundamental variable. Predicted probabilities are generated from logistic regression models regressing the presidential vote on sociodemographic variables (age, race, sex, education, religiosity, income, unemployment) and PIPER for the Full Model. Data points for 1996 are missing, and lines connect 1992 and 2000.

Source: Compiled by authors from the ANES Time Series Cumulative Study, the 2000 ANES Time Series Study, and the 2016 ANES Time Series Study.

FUNDAMENTALS AND THE VOTE, 1952–2020   49

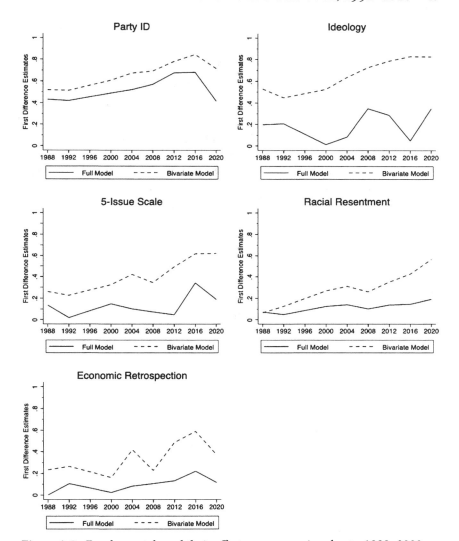

Figure 3.5. Fundamentals and their effect on congressional vote, 1988–2020

Note: Estimates derived by calculating the difference of predicted probabilities at the 25th and 75th percentile values of each fundamental variable. Predicted probabilities are generated from logistic regression models regressing the congressional vote on sociodemographic variables (age, race, sex, education, religiosity, income, unemployment) and PIPER for the Full Model. Data point for 1996 is missing but lines connect 1992 and 2000.

Source: Compiled by authors from the ANES Time Series Cumulative Study, the 2000 ANES Time Series Study, and the 2016 ANES Time Series Study.

50 THE FUNDAMENTAL VOTER

particular fundamental and the vote. That is the total effect of the fundamental on the vote.

Consider party identification first. As Campbell and colleagues would have suspected, it is strongly related to the vote throughout, but even so, up through 2016 its effect had grown marginally but consistently over the elections. In 2020 there was essentially no change in the pair-wise relationship between party identification and the presidential vote, but when considering all the rest of the fundamentals (and SES variables), the effect of partisanship declined substantially. Recall that we observed in the last chapter that the proportion of strong partisans on both sides increased noticeably in 2020, while the proportion of partisan leaners declined, creating a more polarized distribution of partisanship. The increased polarization of partisanship but decreased independent effect of it on the presidential vote suggest that the change in 2020 is due to the stronger relationship (and possibly direct effects) of other fundamentals with partisanship, reducing its independent effects when controlling for the other variables. Perhaps even more so, these findings suggest we need to wait to see whether the 2020 results are lasting.

Compare that with the effect for ideology. Ideology exerts a real effect, one that rivals that of partisanship in some ways, particularly in terms of its total effect. Indeed, it is actually larger in its relationship to the congressional vote than is partisanship. A difference is that controlling for the other fundamentals to estimate the direct effect makes a more substantial difference to the effect size of ideology on the vote than it does for partisanship. Perhaps that is because issues and ideology are tightly linked, as Campbell and colleagues and Converse argued.

Policy, however, reported here using the full, five-item scale, provides a third contrast. Most visually, its effect is one that bounces around considerably over time. While highly variable from election to election, the overall trend is increasing (especially in terms of the total effects measure). Its other pattern is a slowly growing gap between the two lines of total and direct effects. It is striking, therefore, that issues are collectively fairly strongly related to the vote in the twenty-first century (excepting only 2008). Or perhaps more crucially, the point may be how small the effect of policy was between 1988 and 2000. To be sure, the independent effect of issues declined in 2020 from its 2016 counterpart, looking rather similar to partisanship in that regard.

Yet another pattern is found with racial resentment. In both figures, it shows a nearly continually increasing relationship in both ways of looking at it. The racial resentment scale started off fairly modestly related to the vote but has climbed slowly but consistently, such that in 2020 it has an important effect and one that has increased sharply since 2012 in particular. The latter comparison is important because 2012 was the second Obama election and therefore one that we might have imagined had a particularly high racial component. It is also noteworthy that racial resentment was the lone fundamental that increased by both measures in 2020, particularly in the presidential vote, extending the increases observed in 2016. It seems that not only have our elections had an increasing racial component, but this component is somewhat autonomous, increasing even after taking all else into consideration. The increasing influence of racial resentment on either type of vote reaches levels by 2020 comparable to the policy scale, and that means both issues and race are of major influence on the vote, trailing the effects of partisanship and ideology to be sure, but now trailing only by a small margin.

The retrospective economic evaluation question, like the issue scale, also bounces around, here as one should expect, given that the economy changes substantially from election to election.[20] The primary conclusion about its effect on the vote is little more than that it is generally consequential but changes from election to election, and this is especially true for recent elections. Thus, 2020 looks much more like economic retrospection did before the economic turmoil of 2008. Given that the economic effects of COVID appeared well into the 2020 calendar year, it may be that the question aligned poorly with the timing of the sharp changes in economic performance over the year.

We can summarize the role of the fundamentals in 2020 by saying that party identification no longer has as strong and unique an influence on the presidential vote, but it remains the first among equals. Given that 2020 stands in some contrast on all of these measures, we need to wait for results from coming elections to see whether that is a unique feature of 2020 or the start of a trend, with a particular focus on the roles of party and race. Party is thus the fundamental most strongly related to the vote, but by now all of the others are also quite strongly related to the vote. Their combined effect appears, if anything, to outweigh even the substantial effect of partisanship on the vote.

The increased importance of several of the "new" fundamentals is critical to our argument, and we believe that it provides the last important evidence

52 THE FUNDAMENTAL VOTER

of their role as indeed being fundamentals. Perhaps the most interesting change is the growing role of the racial resentment measure, only recently (in the Obama and Trump eras) showing the kinds of relationships we expect for something to be fundamental in orienting the voter to the election. A final important point is that the often-increasing gap between the two measures of effects on the vote suggests that the various fundamentals not only are individually consequential in most cases, but are increasingly related to one another. We will pick up this point later on in this volume, as we make the case for growing electoral-style polarization, perhaps even leading more alarmingly to a growing cleavage in American electoral politics (Chapter 6). We will return to this account soon, but the reader might be interested in knowing just how well these variables together account for the presidential and the congressional votes and how that aspect has changed over time.

The Fundamentals and the Vote

With this backdrop, we can now ask how the fundamentals and SES variables account for the presidential and congressional votes and how this set of relationships has changed over time. As Figure 3.2 indicates, SES variables help shape the fundamentals, which at the time of *The American Voter* meant that they helped shape the only fundamental, party identification. In our view, the SES variables shape all five contemporary fundamentals, which in turn affect short-term evaluations and the vote. We turn to the relationship between the fundamentals and some of the short-term evaluations in the next chapter. Here we are asking how the fundamentals shape the presidential and the congressional votes, regardless of whether short-term factors mediate the relationship, moderate it, or leave it unaffected. Our other major question is how that relationship has changed over the years.

We begin at the beginning. That is, we look first at the relationship between SES variables and the vote directly to see how strongly they are related to how citizens choose. The second step will be to look at the relationship between SES variables and the fundamentals, asking in particular how this relationship combines (in a sort of econometric "final form" sense) to explain the vote. Finally, we will look at the relationship among SES, fundamentals, and voting.

Socioeconomic Status to go along with the Fundamentals

Following the importance of Berelson et al. (1986) and Lazersfeld et al. (1968) demonstration of the foundational role of socioeconomic status on the political psychology of the voter, we composed a set of the "usual suspects" of the social and economic setting of the individual.[21] These are age, race (e.g., White, Black, and Hispanic), gender, education, religion (e.g., Protestant), income, and employment status (e.g., unemployed).

Most of the time we treat these SES variables as "controls" in the fundamentals estimation rather than as estimating the direct and/or indirect effects of any one or all of these variables on subsequent attitudinal or behavioral variables. In particular, we report and discuss a sort of reduced form of a model such as in the Figures 3.4 and 3.5, or more specifically, reporting estimates of the full set of SES variables and the five fundamentals for the years 1988–2020 (except 1996).[22]

Socioeconomic and Other Background Variables and the Vote

If, however, people behave politically as they are socially, to paraphrase Lazarsfeld and colleagues, then we should begin by looking at the overall role these variables play in vote choice. In Figure 3.6 we report the percentage of votes accurately predicted from knowledge of the background variables we use. The two lines in the figure represent one way to assess the total effect of SES on the vote, whether that is the direct effect of, say, race on the vote, or its effect that arises because race shapes the fundamentals, as in the "funnel of causality figure" (Figure 3.2), which in turn more directly determines the vote (sometimes called the "indirect" effect; thus, what we report here is the sum of the direct and indirect effects, hence the "total" effects).

Clearly these social, economic, and demographics variables do help shape the vote. If one flipped a coin as to whether the respondent voted for the Democratic Party or the Republican Party candidate, that random guess would predict correctly 50 percent of the time, on average. In fact, these variables correctly predict between 65 and 70 percent of the presidential vote correctly, election after election, with no obvious time pattern.[23] But even with Trump's efforts to "play the race card," the predictability of the presidential vote returns to its earlier range. The congressional vote is predicted

54   THE FUNDAMENTAL VOTER

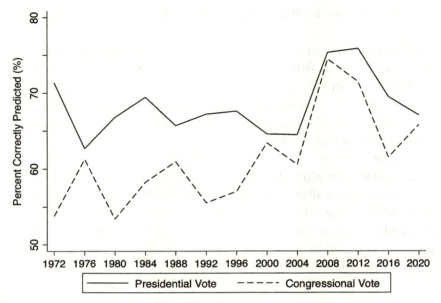

Figure 3.6. Social, economic, and demographic variables and the vote, 1972–2020

Note: Estimates calculated by comparing the actual voting outcomes with predicted probabilities obtained from logistic regression models regressing the presidential or congressional vote on sociodemographic variables (age, race, sex, education, religiosity, income, unemployment).

Source: Compiled by authors from the ANES Time Series Cumulative Study, the 2000 ANES Time Series Study, and the 2016 ANES Time Series Study.

at between 55 and 60 percent of the vote until 2000, at which point it approximates the success found in looking at the presidential vote. One might conclude that the growing similarity between these variables predicting the congressional and the presidential votes provides another indication that the public is increasingly likely to decide their congressional and presidential votes on the same grounds. That is a feature we call the increasing nationalization of the congressional vote.

Predicting something on the order of two in three votes correctly is a clear improvement on random guessing, but as we will see, it pales in comparison to the inclusion of the fundamentals. And except for the five-point or somewhat more increase in predictability of the congressional vote in and around 2000, neither line shows the kinds of changes over time we have come to expect when examining the fundamentals, nor that we will continue to see as we go along. Thus, the SES variables matter, but they take us only so far in understanding electoral choices.

Another way to look at this is in terms of Figure 3.2. In that version of the theory developed by Campbell et al. (1960; note that they never quite endorse this figure, but it is quite close to what they do discuss), all of these variables' effects should be mediated by the fundamentals. How might we know how closely this comes using our data? We first look at the direct relationship between SES and the vote. Then we add our fundamentals to that estimation. If the SES variables decrease in importance in predicting the vote, that indicates that their effect is, at least to that extent, indirect. That is, the SES variables are still important for understanding the basis of the public's vote choices, but they operate to that extent *indirectly* by shaping our five fundamentals, which in turn affect the vote.

We include the details of these two estimations in the online appendix and simply summarize them here. As the data in the appendix illustrate, nearly every one of the SES variables is statistically significant in this prediction in multiple elections for president, and many are in every one; this is almost as true for the congressional vote, especially beginning in 2000. The picture is quite different in the case in which the fundamentals are included along with the SES variables.

The effect of SES on the vote, controlling for the fundamentals, is greatly reduced from what it was with just the SES variables. One way to see this is to look at the reduced extent of these variables being statistically significant in the presence of the fundamentals. The percentage of SES variables significant in the congressional vote equation is originally 41 percent; that drops to 24 percent when the fundamentals are included. The comparable figures for the presidential vote are 40 percent for the total effect, dropping to 26 percent when including the fundamentals. On the other hand, in those same equations for the congressional vote, 72 percent of the fundamental variables are statistically significant, even when including the SES variables, while 95 percent are for the presidential vote. Overall, then, as Campbell and colleagues theorized (but did not directly test), the political importance of where the voter stands socially is strongly (but far from completely) mediated by the fundamentals. That is, socioeconomic status operates politically through its effects on what Campbell and colleagues called the long-term attitudes, which for them reduced simply to partisanship, but are the larger set of fundamentals for us.

56 THE FUNDAMENTAL VOTER

In sum, socioeconomic status helps set the context for the fundamentals and has only modest effects above and beyond that (critical) role. Of course, we consider the fundamentals to be fundamental because they orient the citizen to the electoral politics of the moment and thus to their voting choices. Or at least, so we claim. Let us turn to see how that claim holds up empirically.

The Fundamentals' Relationship to the Vote

We call the model with all five fundamentals the PIPER model, for partisanship, ideology, policy (using the five-issue scale), economic retrospection, and racial resentment. This full model is our basic model for understanding the post-1984 changes in voting behavior. We also report on the relationship between the full set of SES variables and PIP3, the acronym for the three fundamentals available from 1972 to 2020 (partisanship, ideology, and a three-issue policy scale).[24] This is useful to contrast the changing nature of electoral choices before and after 1984. We look at the direct effects of SES and each of the fundamentals on the presidential and congressional votes for the relevant years in this chapter. We consider how they overlap and become increasingly reinforcing of each other and how they are mediated or moderated by some (presumably) short-term attitudes in the next chapter.

The Fundamentals and the Presidential Vote

We will now show how the fundamentals are related to both presidential and congressional voting. We demonstrated in Chapter 1 that the patterns of both presidential and congressional elections appear to have changed beginning in 1984, thus neatly dividing the "ANES era" (1952 onward) in two, with surveys for eight presidential-year elections before 1984 and nine afterward. Innovations in survey methodology and developing theories about electoral behavior, however, mean that our measures of interest only fully came into place in the 1980s. We are able to trace party identification the whole way through from 1952, and we have a consistent and useable measure of ideology and of a small set of issues from 1972 forward, but the other candidates for "fundamental" status began to be measured systematically only in the 1980s. Therefore, we have incomplete measures from 1972 but nearly complete measures from 1988 on. Thus, we are able to track the role of the fundamentals fully for the development of the "new" period in presidential and congressional elections, that is, from the turning point marking the end of the old period in or about 1984 through to 2016. Our core claim is that the fundamental forces underlying voter choice have increased in their collective potency over the post-1984 period, such that even the particular features of the contest at hand are increasingly structured by the reinforcing cleavages of the fundamentals.

First, let us examine the role of the socioeconomic and demographic context and our fundamental forces in shaping the presidential vote.[25] The full model results are presented in the online appendix and will be discussed more fully in the next chapter. We summarize our results in Figure 3.7, which reports the percent correctly predicted by the logit estimation of the fundamentals. We do so sequentially, starting in 1972, when partisanship, ideology, and the smaller set of three issues were included.[26] We include all five fundamentals via PIPER starting in 1988.

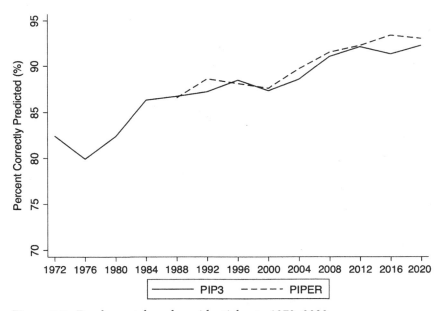

Figure 3.7. Fundamentals and presidential vote, 1972–2020

Note: Estimates calculated by comparing the actual voting outcomes with predicted probabilities obtained from logistic regression models regressing the presidential vote on sociodemographic variables (age, race, sex, education, religiosity, income, unemployment) and PIP3 or PIPER. Data point for 1996 PIPER is missing, and lines connect 1992 and 2000.

Source: Compiled by authors from the ANES Time Series Cumulative Study, the 2000 ANES Time Series Study, and the 2016 ANES Time Series Study.

58 THE FUNDAMENTAL VOTER

There are two obvious conclusions to reach. First, PIP3 does a remarkably good job of "predicting" the vote over the full range of elections from 1972 through 2020. While race, economic retrospection, and the larger set of issues are often quite strongly related to the vote, as we will see later in this chapter, they mostly play a role in dividing up most of the same predictive power as PIP3.

Second, the fundamentals, no matter how they are defined, line up increasingly closely with the vote over time. In 1984, for example, these factors already explained 88 percent of the presidential vote, without any identification of who the candidates were or what made them—or other election specific features—uniquely relevant in that election. By 2016 and 2020, that portion increased to nearly nineteen votes in twenty (or a "proportionate reduction in error" analogue of 50 percent improvement over the period). If we could maintain the notion that these forces shape more short-term evaluations and the vote, but not the reverse, then it is evident that there is very little room for the candidates or other specific features of the campaign to have affected choice substantially and independently. To be sure, the elections were so close that any effect, no matter how minor, could have tipped the balance in 2016 and 2020, but with almost 95 percent of the votes predictable already, campaign and candidate characteristics could swing very few individuals one way or the other away from the choice that their fundamentals pointed them toward.

Finally, we can see how the fundamentals and their role in voting may help us understand the changes in presidential voting. This is especially true for the post-1984 pattern. The fundamentals almost linearly increase in their relationship to the vote, election by election. By 2020 this continuous change has reached something that must necessarily be close to its apogee. The relationship between the fundamentals and the vote has steadily grown step by step to become nearly sufficient alone to account for all presidential votes.

The Fundamentals and the Congressional Vote

Figure 3.8 reports the overall fit of the comparable estimations of the congressional vote. The right-hand side of our model is unchanged, except now the dependent variable is the choice between the Republican and the

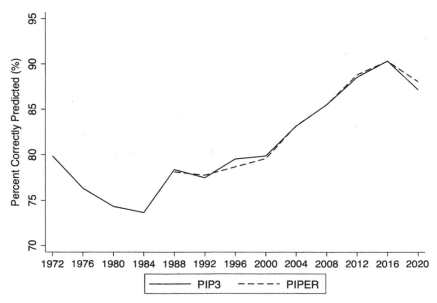

Figure 3.8. Fundamentals and congressional vote, 1972–2020

Note: Estimates calculated by comparing the actual voting outcomes with predicted probabilities obtained from logistic regression models regressing the congressional vote on sociodemographic variables (age, race, sex, education, religiosity, income, unemployment) and PIP3 or PIPER. Data point for 1996 PIPER is missing, and lines connect 1992 and 2000.

Source: Compiled by authors from the ANES Time Series Cumulative Study, the 2000 ANES Time Series Study, and the 2016 ANES Time Series Study.

Democratic House candidates in the respondent's district. Here, the role of the fundamentals has increased, if anything, even more. In 1984, fewer than three votes in four conformed to what the fundamentals forecast. By 2016, over seven in eight were correctly forecast (or a PRE of 56 percent), although it fell back in 2020 to a bit less than the 2012 level. To be sure, incumbents win at very high percentages. But it appears that the reason for their success has shifted from the advantages that accrue to the individual from holding office, per se, to the partisan, policy, and political makeup of the district. Or perhaps more accurately, the basis of congressional choice has shifted back from the advantage held by the personage of the incumbent to the mostly partisan basis for voting that Stokes and Miller (1963) found in the 1950s. The difference is that the partisan basis now includes ideology, issues, race, and the economy within its penumbra.

60 THE FUNDAMENTAL VOTER

Summing It Up: How Electoral Politics Changed from the 1980s through 2020

We have shown several things in this chapter. First, we developed a logic for defining a fundamental, and we proposed that there are five such forces we can measure that meet, more or less closely, that definition. Second, we used the ANES surveys from 1972 through 2020 to provide a means of indicating how those who study elections closely consider each fundamental as a core item for understanding voter choice. Third, we showed that each fundamental is often (but for some measures not always) strongly related to the vote, both by itself and in combination with the other fundamentals. In addition, we found that the fundamentals predict a very large proportion of the presidential and the congressional votes.

Finally, we found that the net effect of the fundamentals has been increasing steadily since the 1980s. This fact helps explain the changing nature of presidential and congressional elections since 1984. That is, the post-1984 period is characterized by an increasing role for the fundamentals and a decreasing role for candidates, such as congressional incumbency or the cross-party appeal of particularly popular presidential candidates (often incumbents) that Stokes found typified the pre-1984 presidential election era. The opportunity for such short-term features of the candidates and their campaigns to change voting choices has been curtailed, nearly step by step, election by election, since the 1980s. And yet partisan coalitions themselves have changed significantly since Reagan was president. A major part of this is understood to be what is called partisan polarization. In the next chapter we will see that this has substantially changed the relationships among the five fundamentals.

We saw earlier in this chapter that the electorate has increased fundamentals' potential for use in electoral behavior, as indicated by the dramatic increase in the public's meeting the conditions long ago outlined for using ideology and issues in voting choices. We also saw how racial attitudes especially have become increasingly strongly related to voting decisions. That is one key part of the explanation of how elections have evolved over the post-1984 period. The second part is how these various fundamentals have increasingly come to reinforce each other. Partisan polarization among the public is the process of sorting the electorate so that a great many more voters today now stand on the same side of all fundamental divisions in politics and stand on the opposite side on virtually all matters of political importance from their partisan opposition. Sorting and its relationship to the public's version of partisan polarization is the subject of the next chapter.

4

The Fundamentals Sort and Polarize the Electorate

In the last two chapters we explained why we believe the range of fundamental forces that orient the public to electoral politics expanded from the single instance of partisan identification in the 1950s to a full set of five such fundamentals by the 2020s.[1] This broadening of the scope of shared means of understanding and evaluating politics has had the effect of making it possible for a typical citizen to bring much more political substance to bear on his or her choice of candidates to support, and quite possibly more emotional charge to the choosing as well, as we explore in the next chapter. We also showed that, especially regarding ideology and a set of durable issues, more voters have become able to employ those orienting forces more frequently, as illustrated by the dramatic growth in the electorate's ability to meet the "conditions" for issue and ideological voting. In Chapter 2 we found that the public's assessment of the economy in retrospect follows reasonably closely the actual path of the economy, indicating that at least this one assessment and possibly others also have a plausible basis in substance. We further showed in Chapter 3 that this combination of broadening and deepening of electoral fundamentals was indeed directly related to candidate and party choice on Election Day. Both presidential and congressional votes have become highly predictable based on knowledge of the voters' responses to these fundamentals, and we have shown that although party identification usually plays the largest role in those choices, each of the fundamentals has a substantial effect on the vote in many elections. In this chapter we pursue our claim that the growth in breadth and depth of fundamentals over the last seventy years has been nearly coincidental with the consideration of partisan polarization in the electorate, because it is the increasingly strong elite partisan polarization on fundamental matters that has made it possible for the typical voter to imbue their partisanship with greater substantive content.

If one observation dominates our understanding of recent trends in American politics, it is that contemporary politics is increasingly polarized

---

The Fundamental Voter. John H. Aldrich, Suhyen Bae, and Bailey K. Sanders, Oxford University Press.
© Oxford University Press 2024. DOI: 10.1093/oso/9780197745489.003.0004

by party.[2] Most people mean by this that it is above all the members of the two parties in Congress who have become polarized, along with other elected officials and party leaders. After all, Congress is where law is made and therefore where polarization would have its greatest effects. Further, partisan polarization was first visible among political elites such as those in Congress, it has continued to increase there since then, and it is often considered to be the reason the public has finally come to be polarized itself, if it is polarized at all.

In this chapter we will see that what most people take polarization to mean in Congress is different from the nature of polarization we find among the public. Indeed, one of the most worrisome aspects of congressional polarization, the growing extremism that separates the two parties, is largely absent among the public.[3] The electorate, we will see, is nonetheless much more greatly polarized in 2020 than it was in, say, the 1970s, due to partisan sorting. We will also see that the sense in which "the electorate is polarizing via sorting" has been occurring about as rapidly in recent years as the Congress polarized in the sense of moving to the extremes over the preceding decades. It is doing so, however, at such a great lag that it is difficult to see how increasing congressional polarization could be *directly* influencing increasing electoral polarization.

Partisan Polarization in Congress

Our interest is in electoral polarization, but to place it in democratic context we need to see what partisan polarization among the political leaders of the nation looks like. And the evidence for its occurrence is clear. We employ one basic measure but show it from several different viewpoints to emphasize different aspects of partisan polarization in Congress.

First, some variant of Figure 4.1 is used by academics and journalists alike to demonstrate partisan polarization in Congress. In that figure we illustrate how far apart the average affiliates of the two parties have been in Congress, year after year, using a set of data that are commonly employed in this regard among academics and method technology called "DW-NOMINATE" created by Poole and Rosenthal (1987; 1997, 2011 as reported at voteview. com), every nonunanimous vote in the history of Congress is used to create a score for every member of Congress.[4] Poole and Rosenthal, like a great majority of academics and reporters, think of this score as how liberal or conservative the member of Congress's votes are.[5] We show this party difference

Figure 4.1. Partisan polarization in US House, 1879–2023
Source: Absolute mean difference in DW-NOMINATE scores between parties obtained from Lewis et al., *Voteview: Congressional Roll-Call Votes Database*, 2023, https://voteview.com.

in the House from 1879—that is, from just after the end of Reconstruction (and completion of reentry of the Confederate states into the nation)—to date. The figure reflects the fact that, as Poole and Rosenthal argue, in the last few decades a single dimension has increasingly defined congressional voting patterns. They find that other dimensions remain relevant, but the first, or what they assess to be an ideological, dimension is increasingly important.

Second, as the figure shows, party differences have waxed and waned over time. Polarization was relatively high in the post-Reconstruction era but then declined throughout the first half of the twentieth century. After it was at that low point for several decades, the parties increasingly polarized beginning around the mid-1970s, and these differences have reached historic highs in recent years. Combined with increasingly close electoral outcomes and (thus) more frequent instances of divided control of the presidency, House, and Senate, gridlock, or the inability to pass legislation, has become increasingly common.[6]

The third point is that underlying this growing partisan division is the fact that the parties have been moving more toward their respective extreme points on this increasingly dominant left-right dimension. We demonstrate this last point using a different way to view the same Poole-Rosenthal data. If the majority party seeks to win passage on the floor, it might try to form a winning coalition by seeking the support of at least 218 of its own members. We measure such a coalition as the distribution of the 218 members of the majority party closest to the center of their party (these data come from Aldrich, Ramjug, and Whyman 2021). We pick 218 because that is the number needed to pass a bill on the floor, so for 2021 and 2022 (i.e., the 117th Congress), we look at the average majority party member and another 217 nearest to him or her, indicating just what a typical majority vote by party would look like.[7] These results are shown in Figure 4.2 from 1877 to date. That figure shows that the two parties have grown increasingly farther apart over the last seventy years, that such divergence has

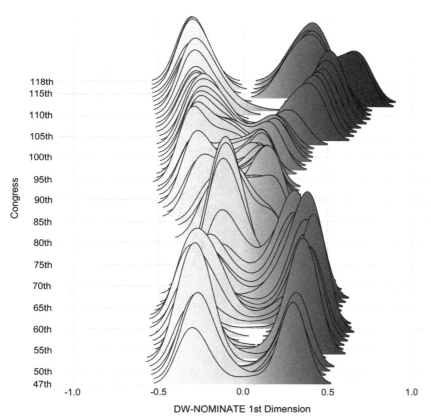

Figure 4.2. Forming party majority in US House, 1879–2023

Note: Distribution of DW-NOMINATE scores of a minimal winning coalition of only majority party members, centered on the majority party median in the House in each Congress. Lighter color denotes Members of Congress just to the left of the median Member on the floor, that is, those voting slightly more liberally than the median, the darker color indicating those to the right, voting slightly more conservative.

Source: Compiled by authors from Lewis et al., *Voteview: Congressional Roll-Call Votes Database*, 2023, https://voteview.com.

66   THE FUNDAMENTAL VOTER

become greater since about 2000, and that the two parties are moving toward their party's extreme. These data are exactly what scholars and journalists alike mean by "increasing polarization in politics today," especially in Congress.

Perhaps, one might say, the two parties are on average far apart, but there might be lots of opportunities to fashion bipartisan coalitions to get bills passed. And indeed, many bills pass Congress with considerably more than 218 votes and often draw at least some support from the minority party. Figure 4.3, however, shows how difficult it has become to create a bipartisan

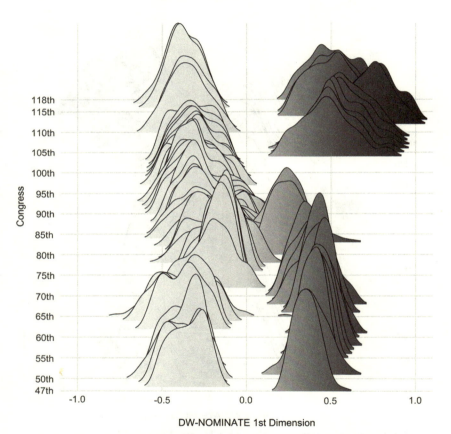

Figure 4.3. Forming centrist majority in US House, 1879–2023

Note: Distribution of DW-NOMINATE scores of a minimal winning majority of House members centered on the floor median in the chamber in each Congress. Lighter color denotes Members of Congress just to the left of the median Member on the floor, darker color indicating those to the right.

Source: Compiled by authors from Lewis et al., *Voteview: Congressional Roll-Call Votes Database*, 2023, https://voteview.com.

coalition in the House. What is reported there is just like in Figure 4.2, except that we report the locations of the 218 most moderate members of Congress in the House, regardless of their party affiliation. That is, we start with the most moderate member of the House and take the 108 MCs just to her or his left and the 108 MCs just to her or his right. While there is somewhat less party distinction in Figure 4.3 than in 4.2, the differences, especially in the last generation, are much less than their similarities. It would be very difficult for a Democratic majority to find enough support in the most moderate wing of the Republican Party to put together even a modest bipartisan coalition, and vice versa for the Republican Party.

There are also substantive reasons for believing that the congressional parties are in fact becoming more extreme. For example, in 1976 incumbent president Gerald R. Ford chose Sen. Robert Dole (R-KS) to be his running mate to provide representation of the more extreme Republican right wing. In 1996 Dole ran for president as leader of the *moderately* conservative wing of his party, in tension with Speaker Newt Gingrich (R-GA) and the much more conservative wing of the Republican Party. And in recent years, Tea Party Republicans and members of the Freedom Caucus in the House seem much more conservative than were (and are) the "Gingrich Republicans" (see, e.g., Theriault 2013), illustrating an increasing rightward move by the GOP. On the Democratic side, the demise of the one-party South effectively eliminated virtually all of the most conservative Democrats, beginning around 1980 or a bit later. Many of the remaining southern Democrats are from heavily minority districts and thus are much more liberal than their erstwhile counterparts were in the era before African Americans could vote. In these ways and more, both parties seem more extreme now than in earlier eras (Theriault 2008; Hetherington 2009; Mann and Ornstein 2012).

Public Perceptions of Congressional Polarization

To begin to connect partisan polarization in Congress with the public, consider Figure 4.4. The dotted line in that figure presents the Poole-Rosenthal data in Figure 4.1 but for just 1952 to 2020, so we can focus on what was happening in Congress during the era for which we have ANES survey data. Convenient for our analyses, the first ANES surveys were in the field when Congress was about at its least polarized. Over time the two parties have been voting more and more on liberal-conservative terms, and the level of voting

68   THE FUNDAMENTAL VOTER

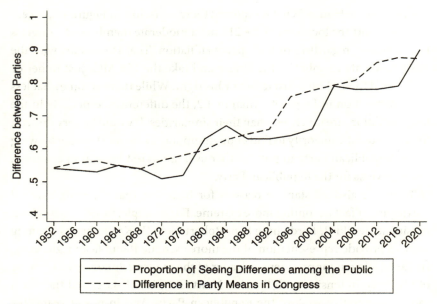

Figure 4.4. Public's perception of party differences, 1952–2020

Note: Data point for 1996 Proportion Seeing Difference among the Public is missing, and line connects 1952 and 1968.

Source: Proportion seeing party differences among the public compiled by authors from the ANES Time Series Cumulative Data File. Difference in Party Means in DW-NOMINATE scores obtained from Lewis et al., *Voteview: Congressional Roll-Call Votes Database*, 2023, https://voteview.com.

along party lines has risen in step with this apparent ideological voting. In particular, there was little change until 1968, at which point partisan polarization in Congress began, followed by a higher rate of polarization starting in 1992. It is on this basis that many conclude that the increasing levels of partisan opposition reflect an increasing extent to which the two parties are diverging from one another toward supporting ever-more-extreme liberal or conservative policy proposals.

Recall that in Chapter 2 we said Converse's explanation (2006) of why he was looking for the presence of a liberal-conservative ideology in his pathbreaking work was that it was the one kind of ideology that might serve to tie the views of public and politician together. While he found too few among the public for that to matter, if ideology (or issues or whatever other fundamental) is increasingly important, then his interest would be rekindled in seeing how the electorate views their officeholders.

This point raises the important question of whether the public observes the increasing partisan polarization of Congress, or its members "waltz before a blind audience," as one might guess would be the case if the electorate were truly nonideological. In fact, the public has not been oblivious to the increase in partisan polarization in Congress. The solid line in Figure 4.4 presents the proportion of the respondents who said that they saw differences between the two parties, along with the actual differences between the two parties.[8] The similarity between these two trend lines is striking. As members of the two parties in fact voted increasingly differently from each other on the floor of Congress, the electorate perceived that increasing difference. The potential for a meaningful dialogue between voters and those whom they elect is thus possible. Or at the very least, members of Congress are not voting in a vacuum, unobserved by the public.

Partisan Polarization in the Electorate

We can now understand why so many people believe that politicians are much more polarized along party lines today than they were in the 1950s. It is not just that they are increasingly separated from each other, but that the Democrats are becoming increasingly extreme liberals, and Republicans are more dramatically becoming increasingly extreme conservatives—and the public notices those facts. What then do we observe about the public's own attitudes? One way to ask the question is whether the distribution of responses to the same questions changes over time or persist as they were at the outset of our data's starting point. Our question here is not whether Democrats and Republicans differ from one another, but whether the public as a whole has become more extreme in its views. We have said that overall the public has only marginally increased its polarization, in the sense of becoming more extreme in its views.

One way to answer this question is to look at changes in the means and standard deviations of each fundamental over time. In Figure 4.5 we report the average values in each election survey of four of the fundamentals (we report on the mean of the fifth fundamental, economic retrospection, shortly). These have all been rescaled so that they run from 0 to 1 and are reported from 1972 on.[9]

Figure 4.5 yields two major conclusions. The first is that the mean value of each fundamental in each election survey hovers near the center of the 0–1

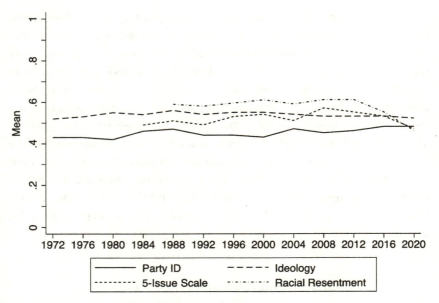

Figure 4.5. Average of four fundamentals, 1972–2020

Note: Data point for 1996 Racial Resentment is missing, and the line connects 1992 and 2000. The 5 Issue Scale line begins in 1984, and the Racial Resentment line begins in 1988 when the relevant questions were first asked.

Source: Compiled by authors from the ANES Time Series Cumulative Data File, the 2000 ANES Time Series Study, and the 2016 ANES Time Series Study.

range. The average respondent, that is, is moderate. Second, the mean score of each fundamental does not vary greatly from election to election for any of these four; indeed, it hardly varies at all.

It is of course possible that individual respondents are typically getting more extreme on these measures over time but are being balanced by others moving toward the opposite extreme, thus keeping these averages about the same. If that were so, it would mean that the movement of one set of respondents, Republicans, say, or conservatives, or the racially resentful, was being offset by a nearly equal number of Democrats/liberals/the racially unresentful becoming just as increasingly extreme in their views, only in the other direction. This is close to what happened at the elite level, leaving a "hollowed out" middle. We can determine whether that is true among the public.

If there were increasing extremity with balanced growth of more extreme liberals and more extreme conservatives, the movement to the extremes

FUNDAMENTALS SORT AND POLARIZE THE ELECTORATE 71

would increase the standard deviation of that particular fundamental over time. As we can see in Figure 4.6 (which includes all five measures), however, that is not the case. The clear evidence is that there is virtually no trend at all in Figure 4.6. At least that is certainly true through 2016. In 2020 there is a bit of an upturn in several of these. We already noted the increase in variation in partisanship, indicating a growth in strong partisans relative to independent and partisan leaners. Racial resentment seems to show an increase as well, but of course as Figure 4.5 shows, that increases as the mean response becomes less resentful. Those changes are quite small to the naked eye, however. We note them primarily because they could be either the first sign of growing extremism in the electorate or a modest "blip" in 2020. The slightness of the 2020 increase, however, is currently best understood simply as that—slight. Therefore, we conclude that there is little evidence of the public becoming polarized in the sense of moving toward the extremes. The American public

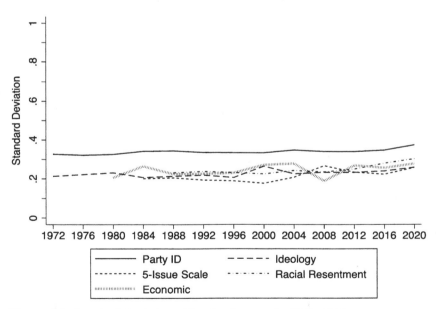

Figure 4.6. Standard deviation of five fundamentals, 1972–2020

Note: Data point for 1996 Racial Resentment is missing, and the line connects 1992 and 2000. The Retrospective Economic Evaluation, the 5 Issue Scale, and the Racial Resentment lines begin in 1980, 1984, and 1988, respectively, when the relevant questions were first asked.

Source: Compiled by authors from the ANES Time Series Cumulative Data File, the 2000 ANES Time Series Study, and the 2016 ANES Time Series Study.

72   THE FUNDAMENTAL VOTER

today is about where it was nearly a half century ago, moderate in most fundamental respects.

To this point we have found that the fundamentals may be described as constant measures yielding consistent responses over time. Focusing specifically on our economic measure, however, does indicate that it has a real and highly variable context. We report the mean and variance of the national economic retrospection variable from its origin in 1980 through 2020 in Figure 4.7. Clearly the average perception of the performance of the national economy changes dramatically over time. In three elections—1980, 1992, and 2008—the mean value is very high (i.e., the average evaluation is very negative). These were indeed the years of actual economic recessions.[10] It is heartening that the public sees those cases "correctly," that is, with a high average account of poor performance, along with correctly calling Reagan's recovery of 1984 (when it was, as his campaign slogan had it, "Morning in America"), the Clinton boom years of 1996 and 2000, and the Obama recovery years of 2012 and 2016. Thus, this measure varies sharply in response to actual economic performance, just as we would hope.

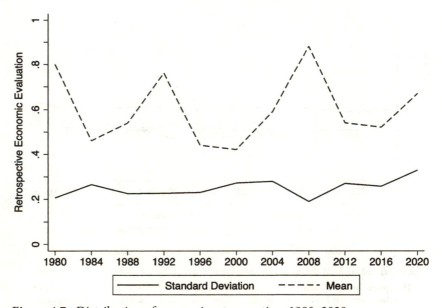

Figure 4.7. Distribution of economic retrospection, 1980–2020

Source: Compiled by authors from the ANES Time Series Cumulative Data File, the 2000 ANES Time Series Study, and the 2016 ANES Time Series Study.

While retrospective views of the economy appear to follow the actual economy, the standard deviation of retrospective national economic performance is rather tranquil amid this stormy sea of average perception of actual performance. The entire electorate, it appears, moves comparably along economic highs and lows, but it is not polarizing over time. If anything, the decrease in this measure over the last four elections, although slight, suggests increasing *consensus* on economic conditions rather than indicating any cross-party dissensus, motivated reasoning, and so on. We are therefore left with the same basic conclusion here as with the other four fundamentals: the electorate is not deeply separated into two competing halves, along party lines or along any other of these fundamental lines. Most have, in the national aggregate, changed little over time, and while the perception of economic performance varies, it does so in coordination with the way the economy itself varies.

The evidence in Figure 4.7, with its varying mean but constant variation in economic retrospection, provides a different pattern, strengthening the case that the public has not grown more extreme on the fundamentals. Ideology, issues, and racial resentment all stayed roughly constant with respect to both mean and variation. The mean of economic retrospection, however, changes quite a bit, meaning that the electorate as a whole has changing views, views that we showed earlier at least partially reflect actual changes in the economy. But the lack of change in the spread of opinion means that the whole distribution stays fixed with respect to observing the true course of the economy. Democrats and Republicans agree that times have gotten better or gotten worse, and they do not change their levels of agreement/disagreement with those views. Thus, even though responses do change over time, there is no reflection of growing partisan disputation of those facts.

We can examine the constancy or change in the electorate's views on the fundamentals one additional way. The 1988 election was near the end of the seesaw pattern for presidential elections and the beginning of the slide toward increasingly and consistently closer elections. Similarly, it was the end of the incumbency-centered congressional election era and the beginning of the growing nationalization of these elections. That is, it was at the end of the old era and just at the beginning of the electoral form of polarization. For its part Congress in 1988 was beginning to show its form of electoral polarization, although of course it has continued to do so through 2020 at least. This was also the first election in which all fundamentals were fully included.

74 THE FUNDAMENTAL VOTER

In Figure 4.8 we report the distribution of the public's responses to partisanship, ideology, the five-issue scale, and racial resentment.[11] The results indicate that any polarization in the sense of growing extremism is very slight and far more muted in the public than at the level of MCs. The public has changed most sharply on two of these, partisanship and racial resentment. Strong partisanship has become the most common response in 2020 (and this is even in comparison with 2016, let alone 1988). Otherwise, the distribution is flat from Weak Democrat to Weak Republican. Given the centrality of partisanship to virtually all theories of American electoral behavior, in the appendix to this chapter we discuss data that have been gathered since the 2020 election concerning partisanship to see what preliminary evidence there might be about its future trajectory, for 2024 and beyond.[12] Racial resentment has changed from a unimodal to a trimodal distribution, with sharp growths at the two extremes and the midpoint being a smaller peak than it was, but nonetheless it is a third mode.[13] Consider, now, ideology. "Pure" moderate ideology remains modal in 2020 as it was in 1988, although there is a slight decline in the proportions. More consequential is an increase in the second-most-extreme category (points 2 and 6) and a general decline in conservatism compared to those placing themselves somewhere on the left. If anything, then, the electorate is uniformly distributed—except for being much rarer at the ideological extremes. The five-item policy scale in 2020 looks quite similar to its 1988 counterpart, with the most notable change being a "flattening" of the scale such that the most moderate category, still the modal category, is lower in 2020 than in 1988, and a consequent modest increase in other categories. In sum, the evidence is that the electorate has not become more extreme in its views on most of the fundamentals, but there is movement toward polarization as more extreme in 2020 (unlike, say, 2016 or earlier) in partisanship and racial resentment.

Electoral Polarization

If the electorate is not following the example of their elected officials and moving toward the extremes to anywhere near the extent their elected officials are, how then might we be observing a different form of polarization in the electorate? What we are observing is an increasing degree of "sorting," such that Democrats are increasingly describing themselves as at least moderately liberal. Republicans are taking at least moderately conservative

FUNDAMENTALS SORT AND POLARIZE THE ELECTORATE 75

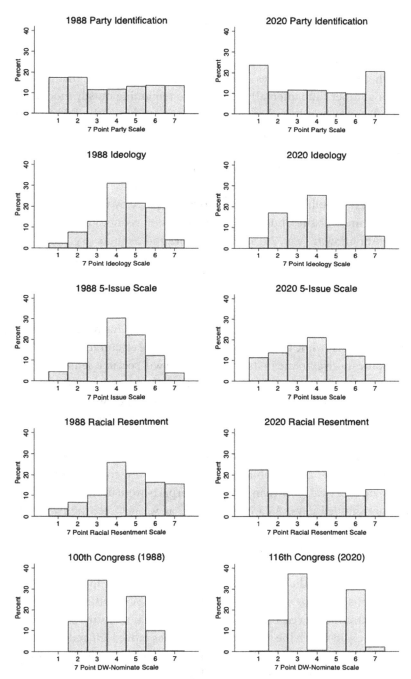

Figure 4.8. Distribution of US House and public on four fundamentals, 1988 and 2020

Source: Compiled by authors from the ANES Time Series Cumulative Data File. Congress's DW-NOMINATE scores obtained from Lewis et al., *Voteview: Congressional Roll-Call Votes Database*, 2023, https://voteview.com.

positions on most issues, racial resentment, and so on. They do so without changing how many liberals and conservatives there are overall. A nearly equal number on one side switch places with an equal number on the other side (whether it is ideologues changing parties or partisans changing ideology or another fundamental), all the while remaining mostly moderate. It is like a deck of cards. Whether sorted by suit or randomly shuffled, there are fifty-two cards, half black and half red. In the 1970s the deck was nearly fully shuffled. In the 2020s it is no longer shuffled but arranged by color. In both cases, there are the same fifty-two cards in the deck, but red cards are now aligned with the other red cards, and black with black.

The idea that political elites are polarized by party by virtue of becoming more extreme on issues, but that the public is not, is one side of a scholarly debate. Abramowitz (e.g., 2013), Abramowitz and Sanders (e.g., 2008), and Campbell (2016), among others, argue that there is, indeed, partisan polarization in the electorate of the sort found in Congress. They argue that partisans in the electorate are farther apart politically from each other than they once were, especially among those citizens most active in politics. In contrast, Fiorina (e.g., 2017), Fiorina et al. (2006), and Levendusky (2009), among others, argue that while there is partisan sorting, the electorate as a whole has not become more extreme in its stances. As we will see, in a sense both sides are right, because sorting means that neither Democrats nor Republicans any longer include large numbers of *both* liberals and conservatives in their ranks. Rather, Democrats consist nearly entirely of moderates and liberals, while Republicans consist nearly entirely of moderates and conservatives. The result is that the average Democrat is now more liberal than in earlier years, and the average Republican has become more conservative, even if they are no more extreme than their counterparts were in the "unsorted" or randomly shuffled days. As a consequence, as we will see, the two parties have indeed grown apart on average, even though the electorate as a whole has changed little, all due to sorting.

We can assess the degree to which a mostly sorting-based partisan polarization has changed the electorate in two ways. The first looks at the consequence of sorting in each of the fundamentals. With little change in the growing extremity of responses (save perhaps racial resentment), sorting is the major way in which the average Democrat has moved left and the average Republican has moved right. We can look at this for ideology, issues, and racial resentment.[14] These are reported in Figure 4.9.

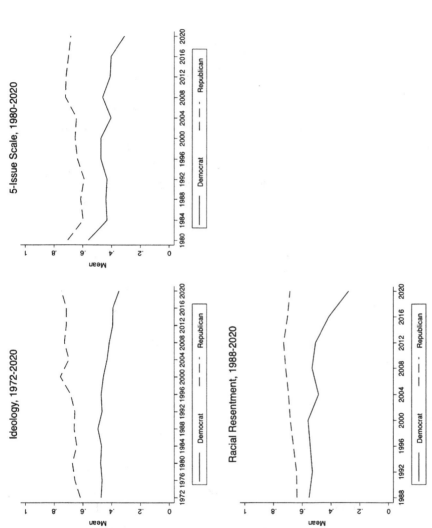

Figure 4.9. Party differences on three fundamentals

Note: Data point for 1996 Racial Resentment is missing, and the line connects 1992 and 2000.

Source: Compiled by authors from the ANES Time Series Cumulative Data File, the 2000 ANES Time Series Study, and the 2016 ANES Time Series Study.

78 THE FUNDAMENTAL VOTER

Each of the three graphs illustrates the point. Sorting alone is sufficient to induce partisan divergence. For ideology, the average Democrat and the average Republican started a more or less slow, steady drift apart from each other, moving toward their respective extremes in the 1980s, a drift that continued at about the same rate through 2020. Its continuous nature meant that by 2020 there was a considerable gap between Democrats and Republicans. Interestingly, it wasn't until 2020 that the average Democrat was clearly (if only slightly) to the left of pure moderation. The set of five seven-point issue scales shows a somewhat different pattern. The average Republican was already conservative in terms of self-placement on them in 1980, when the series begins. After a move to the left, although remaining well on the conservative half of the scale, the average Republican began to drift back to the conservative extreme between 1992 and 2008, at which point they remained about as conservative, on average, as they were in 1980. The Democrats were also net conservative at the beginning but were essentially at the moderate midpoint from 1984 to 2008, at which point they started to move to the left, on average, ending in 2020 very slightly to the left of the moderate midpoint, similar to ideology. By 2020 there is a significantly larger gap between the two parties on issues, as there is on ideology. The same is true for racial resentment, with a much larger gap between the two parties in 2020 than in 1988, when that series began. Here, however, the average Republican has changed little, with a slight but continuous movement toward the more resentful extreme from 1988 to 2012 and then a slight return back toward being less resentful by 2020 (although well on the resentful side, nonetheless). The average Democrat was less resentful than the average Republican in 1988, but not by very much. Starting in 2000, however, they began to move continuously toward the less resentful extreme, moderately at first and then after 2012 much more rapidly. By 2020 the gap is quite large, and change seems to be very heavily due to Democrats becoming much less resentful.[15] The overall consequence of these changes is that the average Democrat stands increasingly distant from the average Republican on electoral fundamentals by 2020, even though the public as a whole is only slightly more extreme than it was. The parties sorted.

The second very important way in which electoral polarization has increased in recent decades is the second consequence of sorting. The data in Figure 4.9 examine how three other fundamentals have changed in their relationship to party identification. But it is not just that Democrats are increasingly commonly on the liberal side on ideology, Republicans increasingly on the conservative side. Rather, it is that all the fundamentals are aligning with each other. What has changed in the electorate, therefore, is that the fundamentals have become more highly correlated with each other. In 1972, for example, the correlation between party identification and self-professed ideology was a fairly modest .32. By 2020 it had increased to a much more substantial and meaningful .71. Whereas in the past many Democrats considered themselves at least somewhat conservative and many Republicans called themselves at least moderately liberal, by now that crosscutting nature of partisanship and ideology has greatly diminished. These two fundamentals now reinforce one another. And as we will see, the move from crosscutting to reinforcing describes all the fundamentals. It is in this sense that voters are polarized.

In past decades the low levels of correlation among these fundamentals meant that one fundamental might push the voter in one direction, while another fundamental might pull them in another direction. The result was that voters' choices might well differ from one election to the next as, say, national economic retrospection might incline a voter to support Carter on the Democratic side in 1976, while the voter's issue preferences might lead her to support Reagan in 1980. By the 2010s and 2020s, however, the fundamentals were much more strongly correlated with each other, and thus, increasingly, they all pulled the voter in more or less the same direction.

Strong evidence for this change can be found in Figures 4.10 and 4.11. In Figure 4.10 we report the pair-wise correlations between the three pairs of fundamentals that make up PIP3, party identification, the seven-point ideology scale, and the combination of the three seven-point policy scales, all asked from 1972 through 2020. The figure shows clearly that all pairs of fundamentals became increasingly and strongly correlated over time. Figure 4.11 reports the average of these pairs of correlations for PIP3 and the comparable average over the five fundamentals that make up PIPER.[16] That figure also demonstrates clearly the pattern of increasing correlation over time, one that extends beyond the PIP3 triumvirate. The average correlation between party, ideology, and our policy scale was under .4 in 1984. By the beginning of the twenty-first century that had increased by about a point, to near .5. In

80   THE FUNDAMENTAL VOTER

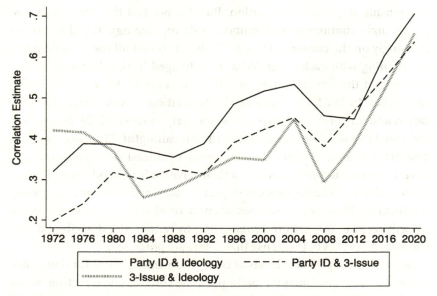

Figure 4.10. Correlations among party, ideology, and issues, 1972–2020

Note: The 1980 Issue Scale is composed for two issue items due to the unavailability of the government health insurance scale question.

Source: Compiled by authors from the ANES Time Series Cumulative Data File, the 2000 ANES Time Series Study, and the 2016 ANES Time Series Study.

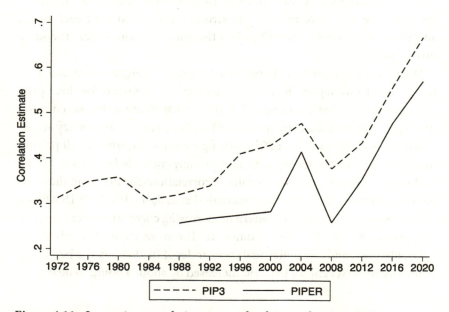

Figure 4.11. Increasing correlation among fundamentals, 1972–2020

Note: Data point for 1996 PIPER is missing, and the line connects 1992 and 2000. The PIPER line begins in 1988 when Racial Resentment was first asked.

Source: Compiled by authors from the ANES Time Series Cumulative Data File, the 2000 ANES Time Series Study, and the 2016 ANES Time Series Study.

2020 it is nearing .7. Adding racial resentment and the economy to the mix yields an average even lower at the beginning, but it increases through 2020 at essentially the same pace as does PIP3. In the context of public opinion and voter behavior research using surveys, this range would go from modest to substantial.

The Two Partisan Polarizations: Political Leadership and General Public

Political elites have polarized by party in two ways. One is that each party is increasingly homogeneous. The second is that the two parties are increasingly diverging from each other and moving toward more extreme positions in either direction. We have seen that the electorate has become more homogenous, like the elites, but not very much more extreme. Thus, while the distributions overall are not getting more extreme, the increasing homogenization within parties via sorting means that the average Democrat will be getting farther away from the average Republican on each of the fundamentals.

What this means is that the two groups of partisans in the electorate should be tracing a path quite like that of partisans as shown in Figure 4.4, that is of the difference between the centers of the two parties in Congress. Figure 4.12 presents such data; that is, it presents the distance separating the average Democrat in the public from the average Republican on ideology, the five-issue scale, and racial resentment.[17] As that figure illustrates, there is a growing differentiation in the public on each of the noneconomic fundamentals. The gentle but continuous increase in each of these from the low points in the 1980s through 2020 is reminiscent of the data in Figure 4.4.

We can make a more direct comparison between partisan polarization in Congress and partisan polarization in the electorate. We can make at least a limited comparison of ideological differentiation between the two parties in Congress and in the public. To be sure, the ideology scale used for the larger public is quite different from Poole and Rosenthal's roll call–based voting scale. To make the comparison between these two different metrics, we rescaled the congressional scores to run 0 to 1, as we have done for the fundamental scales.[18] Given that the developers of the congressional scale refer to it as a measure of ideology, we therefore compare that, over time, to

82 THE FUNDAMENTAL VOTER

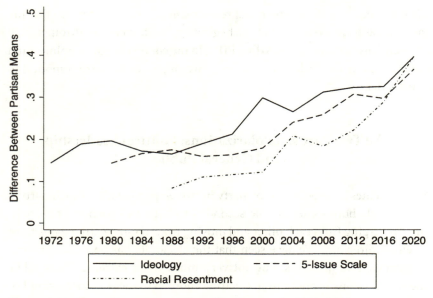

Figure 4.12. Party divergence on three fundamentals, 1972–2020

Note: Data point for 1996 Racial Resentment is missing, and the line connects 1992 and 2000. The 5-Issue Scale was first asked in 1984, and the Racial Resentment questions were first asked in 1988.

Source: Compiled by authors from the ANES Time Series Cumulative Data File, the 2000 ANES Time Series Study, and the 2016 ANES Time Series Study.

the public's self-placements on the ideology scale. We present the results for this elite-mass comparison in Figure 4.13 from 1972 through 2020.[19]

As illustrated in the figure, the distance between the average Democrat and Republican identifier on ideology consistently remains slightly narrower than that for Congress, by about one-half to one-quarter. However, in 2000 the tides turn, signifying a crucial shift marked by an escalation in the distance between partisans in the public surpassing that of congressional polarization. Partisans in the public begin about 0.14 unit apart, increasing to just under 0.4. In 1972, House Democrats and Republicans were about 0.28 unit apart. By now the public stands at about a quarter point larger divergence than the House. The second major observation is that the rate of growth in partisan polarization is slightly higher. That is, the degree to which the electoral parties differ from one another is increasing more rapidly than in the House and therefore exceeds the level observed in the House. A third observation is that both congressional and electoral polarization have been growing since the data begin, in 1972.

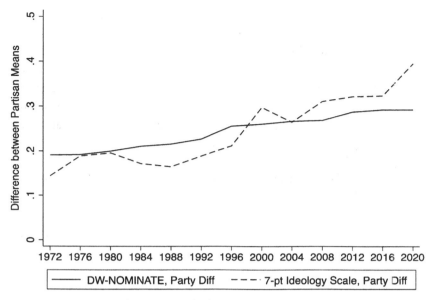

Figure 4.13. Party differences on ideology in US House and public, 1972–2020
Source: Compiled by authors from the ANES Time Series Cumulative Data File, the 2000 ANES Time Series Study, and the 2016 ANES Time Series Study. Congress's DW-NOMINATE scores obtained from Lewis et al., *Voteview: Congressional Roll-Call Votes Database*, https://voteview.com. Both were rescaled to (0,1).

Summing It Up

We opened the chapter by noting that the scholarly and political commentary about American politics in recent decades has been dominated by the growth of partisan polarization. The increasing influence of fundamentals on voting, which we demonstrated in Chapter 3, therefore begs the question of whether the fundamentals are beset by increasing partisan polarization as well. It appears that there is a type of polarization in the public. It does not, however, simply mirror that of elected elites. Rather, it is a distinctively electoral form of polarization, consisting of the polarizing consequences of "sorting" rather than substantial growth in extremism. The striking delayed parallelism between congressional and electoral partisan polarization on ideology leaves open the question of just what the consequences of having a "well-sorted" electorate are and whether sorting simply comes first with growing extremism to follow. We cannot yet address the latter question, but

84   THE FUNDAMENTAL VOTER

the next two chapters do take up questions about the political nature and consequences of these dynamics in the electorate.

In this chapter we have treated the fundamentals as separate measures. Over time, as the public increasingly sorts into partisan, ideological, and policy camps, it seems that the core components of electoral choice are increasingly aligning. In the next chapter we take up the question of how these fundamentals relate to one particular set of short-term attitudes, those relating to the candidates primarily through their emotive or affective content. The growth in negative affect appears to be one of the major consequences of polarization. Therefore, considering this aspect in particular demands attention.

In the sixth chapter we ask whether the electorate, like Congress, is increasingly unidimensional and indeed is best described as divided by a single reinforced cleavage. If this is so, and if this reinforcement includes both affective and, especially, more substantive politics as a part of that cleavage, then partisan camps are increasingly divided by a single, comprehensive cleavage. If so, the second major negative implication is its potential for destabilizing American democracy.

Appendix on Partisanship since 2020

Here we consider in more detail the growing numbers of strong partisan identifiers (in both parties) in 2020, mostly coming with a net reduction in independents who lean toward a party.[20] Having one data point of that sort out of the many we have observed could reflect simple random variation. After all, there are more than forty data points just in Figure 4.6, and having one observation be somewhat larger than the others is something we would expect, and indeed more often than we actually observe, simply by the nature of random sampling. On the other hand, if there were one instance that would be most anticipated to be a substantively significant illustration of growing extremism, it would be party identification in 2020. Is there reality to it? We will consider this question again in the next chapter. Here we note a couple of observations others have made, using data different from ours and from surveys conducted after the 2020 election.

Gallup conducted four surveys measuring its version of party identification in 2021. The surveys do not distinguish between strong and weak partisans, but they found that Democrats and Republicans averaged 56 percent of the respondents, 34 percent were independent leaners, and 8 percent were "pure" independents (Jones 2022). This compares to our 2020 election survey with 67 percent strong and weak partisans, 21 percent "leaning" partisans, and 12 percent pure independents. It is at least possible, then, that 2020 was a particularly "hot" election that made partisans hold their identities even more strongly than usual, but perhaps only for the duration of the election.

Conversely, Pew reports that between 2016 and 2022, extremely negative views of members of the opposition party increased sharply. It asked respondents about five such measures, "Members of the **other** party are a lot" or are "somewhat more closeminded [dishonest] [immoral] [unintelligent] [lazy] than other Americas" (Pew 2022). In 2016, 30 percent of Republicans and 22 percent of Democrats agreed with four or more of those statements, indicating harshly negative views of the opposition. In 2020 comparable percentages were 53 percent for Republicans and 43 percent for Democrats. Granted, the aftermath of the 2020 election and disputation over its outcome have maintained the temperature of electorally relevant politics, if not increased it. Nonetheless, these data suggest that there might be a persistence to this more extreme partisanship that we observe in the 2020 ANES.

The ANES conducted a full, national, online panel survey (from the YouGov panel) shortly after the 2022 congressional elections to pilot test questions for consideration for the 2024 survey. The survey asked the regular party identification battery (modified for online use). It found that there were 20 percent Strong Democrats and 16 percent as Strong Republicans in the sample. Only 10 percent responded as Weak Democrats and 9 percent as Weak Republicans; even fewer, 8 percent, were Independent Democrats and 10 percent Independent Republicans, leaving a much larger than usual 19 percent "pure" independents or coded as "not sure." The decline in "leaners" and the continuing numbers of strong partisans reinforce the Pew data and suggest that the 2020 results were not a one-off oddity, but there are sufficient differences in sampling frame (it cannot be considered a random sample, as is true for all ongoing panels of this sort) and question design to require considerable caution in making those inferences. We must await the 2024 elections to see if the more extreme pattern of responses to partisanship found in 2020 continues in a presidential election year (and with a newly sampled set of respondents).

5

How Fundamentals Shape Evaluations of Candidates and Campaigns

Polarization may be the most intensely studied problem of contemporary American democracy. Right behind it, however, is what most believe to be the most deleterious outgrowth of polarization: the explosion of negative affect toward the political parties, their candidates, and their supporters. Some worry this negativity is a threat to the viability of American democracy. We have seen signs of this in earlier chapters, but here we focus on it more closely. Parties and candidates make up two-thirds of the parties-issues-candidates triumvirate that Campbell et al. (1960) specified as the most proximate attitudes standing just before the voting decision is actually made. We believe, like many, that the affective assessments are surely as consequential as any other component of short-term attitudes.[1]

Lilliana Mason (2018), building on Green et al. (2002) among others,[2] argued that partisanship has become a political identity for a growing number of partisans, in a way that it had not been even in the 1950s when it was originally defined as partisan identification.[3] Associated with that was a claim of increasingly highly charged affect that was coupled with these identities. But it was Iyengar and colleagues (e.g., 2019) who more directly focused on this component of partisanship and who provided a graphical demonstration of negative affect as forcefully as the Poole-Rosenthal (1997, 2011) demonstration of partisan polarization in Congress did. Figure 5.1 makes the case that one of the singularly important features of electoral opinions in the last few decades is the growth of negative assessments of the opposing party and opposing presidential candidates.

In this chapter we move from examination of the fundamentals per se to look more closely at their role in orienting the public toward the electoral politics of the immediate campaign (to paraphrase the authors of *The American Voter*). We then examine the role of these fundamentals in shaping evaluations of what Campbell et al. (1960) referred to as "short-term attitudes," which made up their "components of electoral decisions." We will

---

The Fundamental Voter. John H. Aldrich, Suhyen Bae, and Bailey K. Sanders, Oxford University Press.
© Oxford University Press 2024. DOI: 10.1093/oso/9780197745489.003.0005

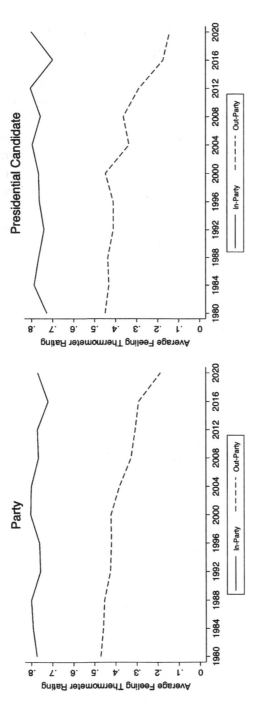

Figure 5.1. Partisan evaluations of parties and presidential candidates, 1980–2020

Note: Estimates obtained from mean values of normalized feeling thermometer ratings of the Democratic and Republican Party and presidential candidates by in-partisans and out-partisans.

Source: Compiled by authors from the ANES Time Series Cumulative Data File.

88 THE FUNDAMENTAL VOTER

assess how the fundamentals shape—and exert their influence on—voting by acting through these more proximate factors. We will show that the change in elections from 1984 onward can be understood in this fashion, as the specific features of the particular contests mediate the growing electoral polarization of the fundamentals in shaping the changing basis of the vote. Unlike Campbell et al., we focus only on candidate- and party-related short-term attitudes, with a special emphasis on what many scholars consider to be the affective or emotional side of attitudes (attitudes can be thought of as consisting of affective and cognitive components). To be sure, the thermometer measures typically used in this regard appear to be related to all kinds of things and thereby seem relevant for understanding cognitive in addition to affective components. But these, particularly the candidate thermometers, are basically short-term measures about the affective components.[4] After all, the thermometer question asks how warmly or coolly the respondent *feels* toward the parties and candidates, not how they *think* about them.

The Importance of Candidate Assessments

Claims by Campbell et al. (1960) about partisanship must have seemed a bit odd at the time. As we noted earlier, if partisanship was so central to their understanding of voting, and if Democrats led Republicans by as much as 60–40 in the 1950s, how could Campbell and colleagues use it as the core fundamental to explain Eisenhower's two presidential victories, which they were writing about, and even the Republicans carrying both the House and Senate in 1952? Stokes (1966) attacked that problem. He argued that the dynamics from one election to another were due to the great variability in how voters assessed the two candidates.[5] Campbell et al. had not argued, after all, that party identification determined evaluations of candidates, only that it helped shape them. And while Stokes did not discuss congressional campaigns in this work, it would not be surprising for him to have said that by "candidates" he meant exactly presidential nominees who were so widely covered and visual on the new medium of television. They were an exception that slid past the typical voter's lack of interest in politics and into public and personal view. After all, congressional candidates, Stokes and Miller (1962) had just shown, were little known except in extreme circumstances. Here we trace developments since the 1950s and early 1960s for both presidential contenders and congressional candidates, particularly relevant in the age of incumbency advantage that followed shortly after Miller and Stokes published.

The Growing Role of the Fundamentals in Congressional Elections since the 1980s

We begin with congressional general elections. Studying congressional voting decisions presents a number of formidable challenges, particularly regarding the role of candidates in voter choice. Although Speaker Tip O'Neill may have been correct at the time when he declared "all [congressional] politics is local," election surveys assuredly are not. While presidential elections are perfectly designed for national surveys (there are usually just two major-party nominees, and every voter faces the same two choices), congressional elections cause headaches for survey methodologists.[6] There are well over 800 different party nominees in 435 unique congressional districts, and thus in any realistic sample very few respondents are drawn from any one congressional district.[7] Thus, it is very difficult to figure out what kind of inferences are possible within a national survey that can provide insight into understanding congressional elections as they happen in individual districts.

In 1978 the ANES held a conference of many of the leading congressional scholars of the time to consider just these sorts of questions. These efforts led to a congressionally focused survey questionnaire. This new instrument was combined with a survey design that featured the congressional district as one of its bases for sampling, implemented only for the surveys of 1978 and 1980. This new, congressionally focused survey showed that a simple set of variables captured a sufficiently large amount of the variation in the nature of candidate choice from district to district. Fortunately for our purposes, these key survey measures have been asked from 1980 onward, so we can see if the broad parameters of local campaign characteristics of the district have changed with respect to their effects on congressional elections throughout the nation since the late 1970s and 1980s. To be sure, these variables fail to capture the full complexity and richness of the local campaign, candidates, and context of 435 congressional races, but they do provide a surprisingly robust first cut.

The first key dimension is incumbency. Is there an incumbent running for re-election in the district? If so, is the incumbent of the voter's party or not? This information by itself should capture a good bit of the differences

90　THE FUNDAMENTAL VOTER

between districts in an incumbency-advantaged era. But of course the campaign features two contenders. Thus, a key dimension of the incumbency advantage was that challengers frequently failed to attract the public's attention at all. So the question of whether there was a heated contest or a one-sided election often turned on whether the voters were familiar with one candidate, both, or maybe neither. We can measure a candidate's ability to garner the public's attention with their ability to respond at all to candidate feeling thermometer questions—it does not bode well for a candidate if many voters are unable to rate him or her on such a thermometer. We call these two sets of variables "incumbency" and "familiarity," following Jacobson and Carson (e.g., 2019).[8] We also follow them in their demonstration that incumbency and familiarity, together, capture enough of the special features and circumstances of the campaign to give us a good idea how much the candidates and districts matter and, equally importantly, how much this aspect has changed over time.[9]

While the ideas of incumbency and familiarity are simple, their measurement is not quite as straightforward: a voter might be faced with no incumbent, an incumbent of their party, an incumbent of the opposition, or (on rare occasions) even two incumbents, for example when they are redistricted into the same district. The voter also might be familiar with neither of the candidates, with their own party's nominee, with that of the opposition, or with both. For this reason, we cannot easily look at the simple bivariate relationship of these variables with the vote. Instead of calculating the "first difference" to measure the size of the effect of a variable on the vote, we look at how the various manifestations of incumbency and familiarity are collectively related to the vote. We consider, that is, the percentage of votes accurately predicted by the combination of incumbency and familiarity. We then compare this net effect with the percentage of votes correctly predicted from just the set of fundamentals, by themselves. Finally, we compare those two sets of percentages with the percentage of cases correctly predicted from all of these variables together, that is, from combining fundamentals and campaign-specific variables.

We begin by reminding ourselves of the effect of fundamentals on the congressional vote from 1972 to date, as shown in Figure 3.8. Recall that the full set of fundamentals (PIPER) is measured only beginning in 1988.[10] We thus plot models including party, ideology, and our three-item issue scale (PIP3) and our full set of the fundamentals (PIPER), respectively. Note first that PIP3, which runs from 1972 on, does most of the work by itself. Expanding policy and adding economic and racial evaluations does not change the basic pattern found with using just PIP3. This suggests that had we had the full set of variables (PIPER) available back to 1972, the story we could tell would likely not be very different than the one we find here.

The most important observation we found in Figure 3.8 was that the fundamentals follow a very clear pattern. In the elections preceding the change in the incumbency advantage in 1984, the fundamentals predict the congressional vote less and less well as the incumbency advantage increases. This changes in 1984. Just as the incumbency advantage was declining, the role of the fundamentals was increasing. It increased steadily after 1984 through the 2012 and 2016 elections. From its low in 1984 of predicting "only" 73 percent of the vote correctly, it increased steadily such that for the two most recent presidential elections, it predicts 88 percent of the congressional vote correctly. This pattern suggests, or at least is consistent with, a story of relatively more local aspects of congressional elections becoming increasingly important into the 1980s before giving way to increasingly nationalized congressional elections.[11]

The predictive power of just the fundamentals, the power of just incumbency and familiarity, and the explanatory power of both the fundamentals and the district-specific measures are presented in Figures 5.2 and 5.3. Figure 5.2 presents the results for 1980–2020 using PIP3, while Figure 5.3 presents the results for 1988–2020 using PIPER.[12] In this way, we can compare the three versions to see how much they help us understand the congressional vote over a longer time period and also for those years with a fuller presentation of the fundamentals.

We ask two questions. What is the effect of the district- and election-specific variables, and how do those district-specific features compare to the effects of the fundamentals in predicting the vote on their own? The answers to these questions are rather clear. Incumbency and familiarity together do a very good job in helping us understand the congressional vote. Their role has, however, decreased over the last few elections. For example, Figure 5.2, with its longer sweep of time for district-specific measures, shows that these variables account for nearly three votes in four. In the new millennium they gradually decrease, until by 2016 they account for fewer than two votes in three. The PIP3 fundamentals start off being quite similar to the district specific measures, but while they turn down after 1988, in both cases the fundamentals grow in importance afterward, to the point where they can be said to explain nearly nine votes in ten.

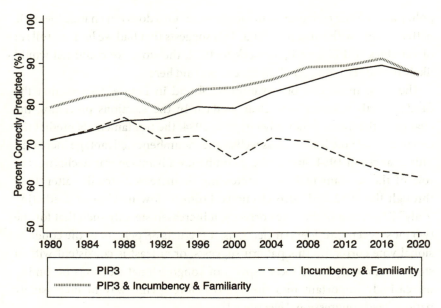

Figure 5.2. Three fundamentals, incumbency, and candidate familiarity predicting congressional vote, 1980–2020

Note: Estimates calculated by comparing the actual voting outcomes with predicted probabilities obtained from logistic regression models regressing congressional vote on PIP3 or candidate incumbency and familiarity, or all three.

Source: Compiled by authors from the ANES Time Series Cumulative Data File, the 2000 ANES Time Series Study, and the 2016 ANES Time Series Study.

How do these two sets of variables together relate to the vote? In this case, the final (and highest) lines in Figures 5.2 and 5.3 provide us with an answer to this question. While both the fundamentals and district-specific variables are strongly related to the vote individually, it appears that the fundamentals carry the greater weight. On their own, they trace nearly the same path over time as does the full set of variables, collectively. To be sure, there is a bit more gained from considering all the measures, but the vote is nearly as well "predicted" from knowledge of the fundamentals as it is from knowledge of the fundamentals, incumbency, and familiarity, all together.[13] Thus, looking at incumbency and familiarity alone provides real insight into the nature of congressional elections, but they are at least modestly (but consistently) declining in that regard. The fundamentals, in contrast, begin at about the same point as the district-specific measures, and their effect on the congressional vote has been modestly but consistently increasing over time. One could

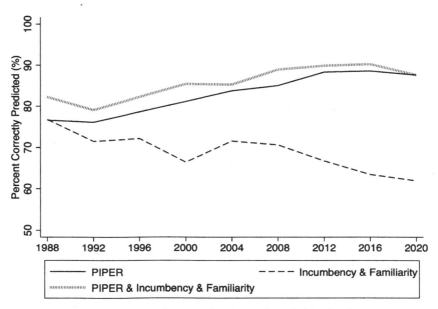

Figure 5.3. Five fundamentals, incumbency, and candidate familiarity predicting congressional vote, 1988–2020

Note: Estimates calculated by comparing the actual voting outcomes with predicted probabilities generated from logistic regression models regressing congressional vote on PIPER or candidate incumbency and familiarity, or all three. Data points for 1996 PIPER and 1996 PIPER & Incumbency & Familiarity are missing, and the lines connect 1992 and 2000.

Source: Compiled by authors from the ANES Time Series Cumulative Data File, the 2000 ANES Time Series Study, and the 2016 ANES Time Series Study.

infer that incumbency and familiarity add little to the overall account.[14] We therefore conclude that the congressional vote is almost certainly determined more fully by national considerations and that the decline in incumbency advantage is mirrored in the decline in the influence of the candidates and other district-specific features.

How the Fundamentals Affect Presidential Evaluations: The Primary Season

We begin our consideration of presidential evaluations by looking at the changes in partisan evaluations of nomination contenders very early in the nomination campaign. We have the good fortune to be able to use full ANES surveys conducted around the time of the first event in presidential nomination contests, the Iowa caucus, in 1980 and then again in 2016. The former is nearing the transition point of 1984 and should be based on a period of a low degree of polarization among the fundamentals shaping how voters think about the presidential candidates in the early days of the primary season. The latter should be well into not only the period of congressional partisan polarization but also the era of electoral-style polarization.

It is also fortunate that the two contests were broadly similar. Two major Democrats competed in the two years. In 1980 James E. "Jimmy" Carter, incumbent president and a moderate Democrat, and Sen. Edward M. "Ted" Kennedy (MA), the leader of the liberal wing of the Democratic Party, ran for nomination. In 2016 former secretary of state Hillary R. Clinton, who had served in the incumbent Obama administration and was a relatively moderate Democrat, ran, as did Sen. Bernie Sanders (I/D, VT) who was a major (and perhaps the most prominent) leader of the progressive wing of the party.

In both years, a great many Republicans ran for the nomination, and we focus on three of the more well-known candidates in each year. In 1980 these were eventual nominee Ronald Reagan (CA), eventual vice-presidential nominee George H. W. Bush, and Sen. Robert Dole, vice-presidential nominee four years earlier in 1980. The 2016 Republican nomination candidates were eventual nominee Donald Trump, Sen. Ted Cruz (TX), and Sen. Marco A. Rubio (FL).

We provide two kinds of results. We first show that the underlying fundamentals were more important in shaping candidate evaluations early in the election season in 2016 than in 1980, and that was true whether the candidates were well known or little known. In results reported in Figure 5.4, we are able to include the same set of demographics and three of the five fundamentals (party identification, ideology, and retrospective economic evaluations) that are used in the analysis of general election surveys. Because we are assessing responses to a one-hundred-point scale, regression is suitable, and thus we report the R-squared value in the figure, a measure of the overall fit of these variables to the thermometer scores.[15] The overall explanatory value of the fundamentals is quite different in the two years. For Democrats and Republicans alike, evaluations in 1980 were simply less well-grounded in the fundamentals than they were in 2016. On the Republican side, the fundamentals contribute less to understanding the public's evaluations than they do in 2016, even though the 2016 candidates were less well-known to the public (Cruz and Rubio) or at least not well-known as a politician (Trump) than their counterparts in 1980. Even though Carter and

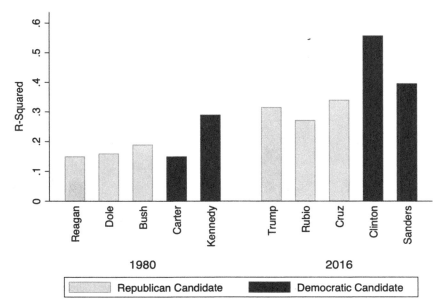

Figure 5.4. Fundamentals and evaluation of presidential nomination candidates by party, 1980 and 2016

Note: R-squared estimates obtained from linear regression models regressing feeling thermometer scores of presidential candidates on sociodemographic variables (age, race, sex, education, income, unemployment) and the fundamental variables (party identification, ideology, retrospective economic evaluation).

Source: Compiled by authors from the 1980 ANES Major Panel Study and the 2016 ANES Pilot Study.

Kennedy were perhaps the two most well-known politicians in the country in 1980, the fundamentals shaped evaluations less than they did for either Clinton or Sanders in 2016.

Our second observation concerns partisan polarization. In Figure 5.5 we report the percentage of Democrats who rated Republican candidates at more than 50 degrees (the midpoint, i.e., the change from "cool" to "warm" ratings) on the one-hundred-point "feeling" thermometer, and vice versa for the Republicans' ratings of Democratic candidates. If there are negative feelings across party lines, that should be reflected in negative evaluations of their candidates. In 1980 major candidates in both parties, incumbent president Carter and soon-to-be-elected vice president George H. W. Bush, were rated warmly by at least half of the opposition party identifiers. In 2016, by contrast, no candidate was rated that warmly by even a quarter of the opposition

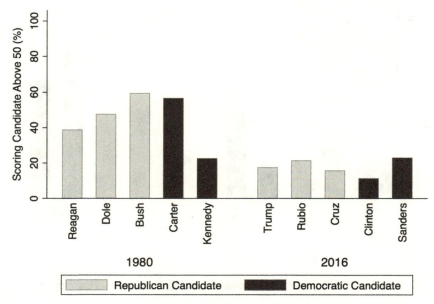

Figure 5.5. Percentage of partisans rating presidential nomination candidates of the opposing party "warmly" by party, 1980 and 2016

Note: Estimates represent the percentage of respondents who gave a feeling thermometer score greater than 50 to out-partisan presidential candidates.

Source: Compiled by authors from the 1980 ANES Major Panel Study and the 2016 ANES Pilot Study.

party identifiers, and the *most* polarizing figure in 1980 (Sen. Ted Kennedy, D-MA) was as warmly received by Republicans as the *least* polarizing candidate was by the opposition in 2016.[16] Thus, we conclude, partisans reacted to the opposing party's candidates (often before knowing much about them individually) with greater negative affect in recent elections, or at least in 2016, than they did in 1980.

Let us return to the role of the various fundamentals. In the online appendix, we report on the full estimation. Here, in Figure 5.6 for Democrats and Figure 5.7 for Republicans, we compare the two elections with respect to the difference that each of the three fundamentals made in the evaluation of the candidates in the two parties. These results lead, first, to the conclusion that partisanship is obviously an important influence on who liked and disliked which candidates in both parties in both years. On the other hand, partisanship was clearly much more strongly related to evaluations of nearly all candidates in 2016 than of those in 1980. Our second fundamental,

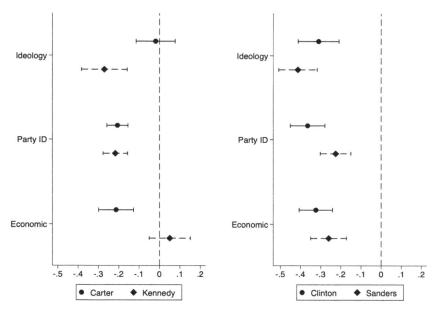

Figure 5.6. Effect of fundamentals on Democratic candidate evaluations, 1980 and 2016

Note: Linear regression models predicting feeling thermometer scores of presidential candidates based on sociodemographic variables (age, race, sex, education, income, unemployment) and the fundamentals (party identification, ideology, retrospective economic evaluation).

Source: Compiled by authors from the 1980 ANES Major Panel Study and the 2016 ANES Pilot Study.

ideology, was also significant in both election years and also much more strongly and consistently so in 2016.[17] Finally, the economy was more important in evaluating the Democrats in 2016 than in 1980, even though the economy was faring especially poorly in 1980 and not nearly so badly in 2016. Carter could well have been held responsible for economic circumstances in his renomination campaign, as he appeared to be in the fall.[18] While significant in some cases, economic retrospection seemed less influential on the Republican side, as one might expect for the party that is not holding the presidency. It appears, in sum, that (1) the fundamentals as a whole were more important in 2016 than in 1980, (2) this was apparently true uniformly across each fundamental, and (3) the electorate is using the fundamentals in sensible ways to reach those evaluations.

We can go several steps further. The 2016 survey happened to include a number of questions that tapped into reactions to the specific circumstances

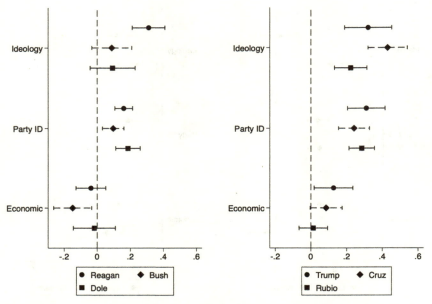

Figure 5.7. Effect of fundamentals on Republican candidate evaluations, 1980 and 2016

Note: Linear regression models predicting feeling thermometer scores of presidential candidates based on sociodemographic variables (age, race, sex, education, income, unemployment) and the fundamentals (party identification, ideology, retrospective economic evaluation).

Source: Compiled by authors from the 1980 ANES Major Panel Study and the 2016 ANES Pilot Study.

and candidates in that election. Even the most casual observer of that election could not help but be aware of how distinctive the two candidates were and the special circumstances they faced. Moreover, these special features were not obviously closely related to the fundamentals. We can ask and partially but more fully than usual answer the question: What, if anything, was uniquely important in 2016? We first look back at the comparison of the two early-nomination period surveys in 1980 and 2016 and then at the general election of that year.

Consider the nomination surveys, as reported above. Note first that our results show the role of the fundamentals was generally similar across all candidates in both parties. That is, partisanship, ideology, and economic evaluations affected all Republicans in the same way and, although in the opposite direction, were similar for both Democrats as well.[19] Note also that Trump in particular does not look especially distinctive from his opponents on the Republican side in 2016. To be sure, partisanship has a slightly stronger effect on his evaluations than it does for other Republicans, but the important point is that such differences are neither large nor unique to Trump. It is simply the case that these three fundamentals were important in understanding evaluations of all candidates.

One exception to these two points does make Trump's support unique. The racial resentment scale was included in the 2016 survey but not in 1980. Including it, we find, first, that it adds to the explanation of evaluations of Trump but also to evaluations of Sanders.[20] Second, its effect was very large for Trump—the racially resentful were much more positively inclined toward him.[21] The nonresentful respondents rated Clinton more highly than did the more resentful, but the nonresentful were substantially more receptive to Sanders.[22] Finally, including racial resentment only had minor consequences for the effects of other variables for all candidates (including Sanders) except for Trump. Adding racial resentment cuts the effect of ideology in Trump evaluations in half, while the effect of economic evaluations drops nearly to zero. Thus, for Trump it appears that racial resentment is the most important fundamental, followed at a fair distance by partisanship, and both ideology and economic evaluations are far less consequential for understanding Trump's attraction.[23]

How the Fundamentals Affect Presidential Evaluations in the General Election

The Role of Specific Features of the 2016 Presidential Election

While electoral polarization made a big difference between early 1980 and early 2016, the makeup of the particular candidates contesting for nomination was relatively less important. In terms relevant to 2016, at first it seemed that evaluations of Trump were pretty much cookie cutter standard for any Republican. Being able to add the racial resentment scale in early 2016, however, did reshuffle considerably just what seemed to matter—racial resentment was what made considerations of Trump's candidacy unique. Before we turn to a full consideration of the role of fundamentals in presidential general elections, might we find a comparable difference in the fall of 2016?

100 THE FUNDAMENTAL VOTER

We consider a wide range of the most commonly given accounts of the 2016 campaign, especially those suggesting it differed from others. After all, most analysts interpreted the presidential campaign as special, even extraordinary. While we cannot examine every aspect of the campaign, we are fortunate that the ANES was able to include at least one and sometimes a substantial number of questions to evaluate some of the most prominent explanations proffered by observers.

Populism, for instance, was a go-to explanation for many pundits.[24] Many viewed Sanders and Trump as tapping into widespread frustrations with the elites and the establishment, picking up voters who felt dismissed by politicians—of either party—in Washington. Following procedures outlined in Aldrich et al. (2019), we are able to tap into a number of dimensions of populist sentiment with various ANES questions.[25] First, economic anxiety is associated with attraction to populism and populist candidates and parties. It is not surprising then, given the slow growth out of the Great Recession of 2008, that economic anxiety also featured prominently in accounts of the contest.[26] It is perfectly reasonable, for example, to imagine respondents saying that the economy is better today than in the recent past, as the fundamental about the economy indicates, and yet say that their family's finances are a source of anxiety and worry. Second, populists often claim that political elites are untrustworthy, and the ANES included a question tapping into that concern.[27] Third, many argue that those described as having an authoritarian personality or at least being susceptible to authoritarianism find populist parties and candidates especially attractive. The ANES has for some time followed the relevant literature by asking a series of questions about attitudes toward childrearing that have been shown to be closely related to authoritarianism.[28]

We also consider the role anti-immigration sentiment may have played in 2016. Trump declared his candidacy (June 16, 2015) by talking in part about immigration and building a wall on the southern border:

The U.S. has become a dumping ground for everybody else's problems. Thank you. It's true, and these are the best and the finest. When Mexico sends its people, they're not sending their best. They're not sending you. They're not sending you. They're sending people that have lots of problems, and they're bringing those problems with us. They're bringing drugs. They're bringing crime. They're rapists. And some, I assume, are good people. [And later in the speech:] I would build a great wall, and nobody builds walls better than me, believe me, and I'll build them very inexpensively, I will build a great, great wall on our southern border. And I will have Mexico pay for that wall. (Time Staff 2015)

Fortunately the ANES included the module of questions created by the Comparative Study of Electoral Systems (CSES) that tapped into anti-immigration questions, and we can employ them to determine whether or not anti-immigrant sentiment really was a defining aspect of the election.[29]

Finally, Trump has a long history of saying awkward and offensive things about women, and he continued to make such remarks throughout his campaign. For instance, after the first debate among Republican candidates, during which then Fox journalist Megyn Kelly pushed Trump on the topic of sexism, Trump seemed to call Kelly a "bimbo" on Twitter (Cohen 2020). Given that Trump was facing the first female major-party presidential nominee, we could well imagine that attitudes about women influenced voters' choice. The analogue to the racial resentment scale for sexism is called the "modern sexism" scale, and the ANES includes a three-item version of it.[30] Significantly, the ANES also included a question[31] about reactions to the now-infamous *Access Hollywood* video, in which Trump was recorded having an "extremely lewd" conversation in 2005 (Cohen 2020).

While more details are available in the online appendix, we first consider the analysis of each of these explanations embedded in the equation that includes the fundamentals. The estimates from the full model are reported in Figure 5.8. The results are quite striking. Most aspects of populism (along with the modern sexism scale) are not significantly related to the vote in 2016. Two of the election-specific measures do appear to play a significant role, however. First, anti-immigration sentiment is strongly related to the vote in pairwise comparison. Its coefficient is large and statistically significant. Those respondents who indicated they were opposed to immigration were considerably more likely to vote for Trump than for Clinton, quite as one might expect from a candidate who opened his campaign for the presidency with a speech about immigrant threat. Second, attitudes concerning the *Access Hollywood* video had a very large and both statistically and substantively significant effect on the vote, controlling for nearly everything imaginable. Those who found the *Access Hollywood* video to be important were significantly less likely to vote for Trump.

We can consider these election-specific factors in another way. In Table 5.1 we report the results of the full set of fundamentals and sociodemographic

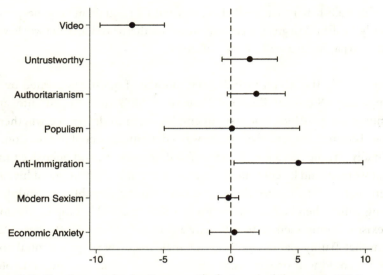

Figure 5.8. Fundamentals, election-specific factors, and the vote in 2016

Note: Logistic regression model predicting the presidential vote. Sociodemographic variables (age, race, sex, education, religiosity, income, unemployment) and the fundamentals (party identification, ideology, 5-issue scale, retrospective economic evaluation, racial resentment) omitted from the figure but included in the model.

Source: Compiled by authors from the 2016 ANES Time Series Study.

Table 5.1. Effects of Campaign-Specific Variables on Evaluations of Candidates in 2016

	Vote Choice (% Correct)	Dem Feeling (R2)	Rep Feeling (R2)
Baseline model	93.44	.677	.598
+Personal economic anxiety	93.28	.678	.598
+Authoritarianism	93.58	.677	.603
+Political distrust	93.43	.690	.60
+Modern sexism	94.43	.677	.598
+Anti-immigrant	93.73	.677	.621
+Trump video matters	95.22	.719	.659

Source: Compiled by authors from the 2016 ANES Time Series Study.

variables on the two candidate-thermometer scores, then add sequentially each of the individual measures for the campaign. We compare the overall fit of the models (the R^2) between the two candidates. We also report the percent correctly predicted for using the same measures in the vote choice equation. Note that just as in the primary season, thermometer evaluations of Clinton were better explained than those of Trump, and by a substantial amount. The additional question is whether knowing about any one of these measures substantially improves the overall understanding of the model, as indicated by a noticeable increase in R^2 (percent correct), and whether these findings differ between the two candidates.

Given the low and often insignificant effects of many of these campaign-specific variables, it is not surprising that the overall fit changed very little. In each case, one variable had a small but noticeable increase for each candidate—but it was a different variable for each. For Clinton, trust (or often, distrust) of political figures increased the explanatory value of her thermometer evaluation, while it had virtually no effect on Trump's. Conversely, the anti-immigration variable was inconsequential for the Clinton variable, but it clearly added a fair amount to Trump's. The big "splash" comes, however, with respect to the *Access Hollywood* video, and this was true for both candidates (in opposite directions, of course). While the effect is quite large for Clinton, it is even more so for Trump. Here, unquestionably, was a campaign-related event that mattered, and it mattered a great deal.

Affective Polarization and the Fundamentals

We continue our consideration of evaluations of the presidential candidates with a look at one of the most intriguing sets of findings in the literature in recent years. As noted earlier, today's story of partisan identification is one of a deeply rooted social identity with large affective components that shape evaluations of the candidates, especially negative evaluations of the opposing candidate. In the 1950s, everyone could and did like Ike—and at various moments, such as their landslide victories, Johnson and Nixon and Reagan— and everyone could dislike Barry M. Goldwater or George McGovern in late 1964 and 1972, respectively. Today that would be true on the positive side only for party identifiers, and on the negative side only for the opposing party's identifiers. And this is so because so many "sorted" partisans like their nominee and dislike the opposing nominee on party, on issues, on ideology, on race, and on evaluations of the economy.

Through 1984, if the public as a whole liked the incumbent, he was likely to win by a landslide. If the public did not, they turned the incumbent out with bipartisan agreement, as they did Ford and Carter. Today, partisans defect from that identification far less often and tend to vote along party lines, making both nonincumbent and incumbent races close and not at all bipartisan. This is the "affective polarization" account of Iyengar et al. (2019), as seen in Figure 5.1.

Consider Figure 5.9, which reports the average thermometer ratings of both the opposition party and the opposition party's candidate from 1980 onward. In the two Reagan elections, each party was only very modestly negative about the opposing party, averaging a rating of forty-five degrees or higher. That near neutrality sagged almost linearly through to 2000, but the decline was slight, dropping to only around forty degrees. But then the decline became precipitous on both sides, with Democrats and Republicans

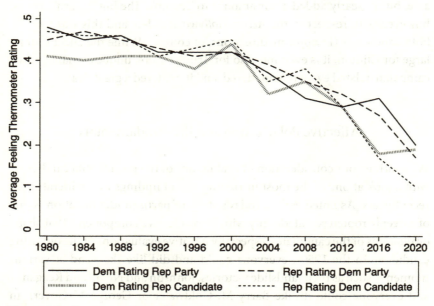

Figure 5.9. Partisan ratings of opposing party and opposing party candidates, 1980–2020

Note: Estimates obtained from mean values of normalized feeling thermometer ratings of the Democratic and Republican Parties and presidential candidates by out-partisans.

Source: Compiled by authors from the ANES Time Series Cumulative Data File.

increasingly reporting cold attitudes toward their opposing partisans. And the drop in evaluations of the opposing candidates is even more stark. While it appeared first in 2012, by 2016 both Trump and Clinton evaluations by the opposition had dropped into the teens. In 2020, both parties were liked by the opposing side even less than in 2016. Trump was evaluated about the same by Democrats in 2020 as in 2016, but Republicans evaluated Biden remarkably negatively, even more so than the previous low evaluations accorded to Clinton in 2016.

The Fundamentals and Candidate Traits

The story outlined above is, of course, a much different account of partisanship and candidate evaluations than that of the 1950s and 1960s. The original story was one of party identification as the exclusive long-term force in orienting the public to electoral politics. It was largely devoid of content, lacking issue or ideological structures to give it substantive meaning. It was learned early in life and helped shape the evaluation of matters that were closer to the individual's vote choice. However, that left great latitude for very large swings from one election to the next in voters' attitudes and choices, driven by massive variation in evaluation of the two parties' nominees from year to year. Such evaluations would be correlated with partisanship, but the effect was largely bipartisan, as Stokes (1966) showed.

The question for us to consider, then, is whether or not the characteristics that the candidates bring to the contest continue to play the important role Stokes (and his coauthors) argued for in earlier decades. We do so by turning, once again, to the ANES.

Starting in 1980, the ANES added a battery of questions seeking to provide more systematic measurement of how citizens evaluate presidential candidates. Drawing from person-perception in psychology, the battery asks how well various traits describe each of the two presidential candidates (Abelson et al. 1982; Kinder 1983b).[32] These trait measures have been found to be strongly related to both overall candidate evaluations and the vote. They are also highly variable from election to election as the parties select different presidential nominees with differing strengths and weaknesses. What matters in terms of choice between the two is the *difference* in the particular trait evaluation. For example, does a voter view Clinton to be a stronger leader than Trump, or as a weaker leader, or does the voter see no difference between the two? Using the three trait

106 THE FUNDAMENTAL VOTER

measures that are included in the ANES most consistently, we calculated the difference between the respondent's assessment of the candidates on each trait and created an average score for each year on a 0 to 1 scale, with higher values indicating that the respondent tended to rate the Republican candidate more positively on each trait. This variable should be strongly related to the vote.

Given that the trait measures were drawn from the social psychology literature on person-perception, they would seem to be the epitome of candidate-specific assessments. And it is certainly true that these are asked about specific individuals and make little sense if not asked in that way. The president, however, is both a person and an office. Further, while we can often assess whether a person is a strong leader, and so on, these three traits are especially important for evaluating someone we are considering voting for to be the next president. That is, these are traits of *special* relevance for the person who holds the office of president.

We could imagine, then, that when voters evaluate a candidate's leadership, compassion, and knowledge, they are thinking about these qualities in terms of the requirements of the institution of the presidency. For instance, a voter who considers whether or not Hillary Clinton is a strong leader is likely thinking about Clinton's ability to lead from the White House, rather than as the leader of the campaign for women's rights around the world, even though she was that. A voter who considers Trump's knowledge base is likely thinking about whether or not he knows enough to make the tough decisions the presidency often calls for, rather than if he knows enough about business or who would make a good apprentice. In this sense, these trait evaluations are a fundamental assessment, and they differ from the other measures we call "fundamental" in two important ways.

One is that each ties the specific features of the individual to the expectations of the office.[33] The other fundamentals did not address the candidates at all, at least not directly and not by name. Another is that our fundamentals are about the way the two parties divide over public policies and the like to indicate why someone should vote for their party and not the opposition. Those fundamentals earn their name because they seek to measure what is fundamental to making a choice in the voting booth. The candidate traits, on the other hand, are about a different political institution: the presidency. Surely how people conceptualize the institution of the presidency should matter in their considerations of who should hold that office, just as their understanding of the institutions of electoral and party systems should matter. And there is no reason to imagine that only Democrats care about the public or that only Republicans can be strong leaders.[34]

We begin our analysis as we did with the congressional vote by refreshing our memory of the relationship between the fundamentals and the presidential vote in Figure 3.7. As before, PIP3 and PIPER trace out a pattern that only modestly alters over time. While 1972 is just a bit higher than 1976, from that 1976 "low" of eight in ten votes correctly predicted, there is a continuous, nearly linear, increase in this measure through to 2020, in which it peaks at more than nine in ten votes correctly predicted.

What happens if we examine the effect of adding the trait measure to our previously discussed account of the fundamentals? Three questions guide our investigation. First, how much of a difference does adding the trait measure make in our ability to predict (empirically explain) the vote, compared to what we could do with just the fundamentals? Consider Figure 5.10. In that

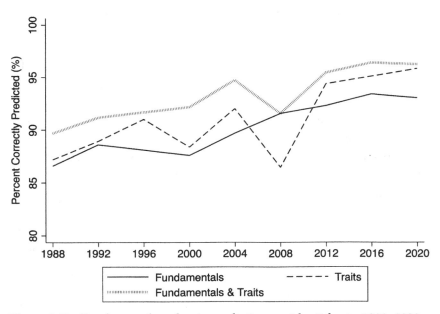

Figure 5.10. Fundamentals and traits predicting presidential vote, 1988–2020

Note: Estimates calculated by comparing the actual voting outcomes with predicted probabilities generated from logistic regression models regressing presidential vote choice on sociodemographic variables (age, race, sex, education, income, unemployment, religiosity) and the fundamentals (party identification, ideology, 5-item policy scale, retrospective economic evaluation, racial resentment) or candidate trait variables (see text), or both. Data points for 1996 Fundamentals and 1996 Fundamental & Traits are missing, and the lines connect 1992 and 2000.

Source: Compiled by authors from the ANES Time Series Cumulative Data File, the 2000 ANES Time Series Study, and the 2016 ANES Time Series Study. Candidate trait variables for 2012 and 2020 obtained from the 2012 ANES Time Series Study and the 2020 ANES Time Series Study.

108   THE FUNDAMENTAL VOTER

figure, we include the percent of votes correctly predicted from knowing just the fundamentals, from knowing just the trait score, and from knowing both the fundamentals and the traits.

We can see a difference between the predictability of the vote from just the fundamentals compared to that from knowledge of just the traits, but only a very modest difference.[35] The two trace a very similar line over time, with a few more ups and downs for the traits, but even that variation is limited. The bottom line is that the two are equally—and very—powerful. Because one is measuring longer term and non-candidate-specific orientations to politics, and the other is closely attached to the candidates of the contest by name, we might expect the two to combine to improve our understanding of the vote even more than when they are considered separately.

Combining the trait variable with the fundamentals adds only an additional 1–3 percent of the vote correctly predicted to that of the fundamentals alone (or equally so when compared to just the traits alone). Of course, each of these is so closely related to the vote that there is very little left to be gained by adding another variable. Moreover, that gain appears to be located primarily before 2008. Since then, considering only traits, or only the fundamentals, or both together makes little difference. In that sense, it is clearly the case that including the trait variable increases our explanation, but it does so only by a very modest amount—and of course the same is true if we started with the traits and added the fundamentals.

An obvious possible explanation for the high degree of overlap in Figure 5.10 is that partisans and/or ideologues might be using some or all of their fundamentals to reach judgments about the opposition and their party's (their ideological group's, etc.) nominees to assess the candidates' traits. We can look to Figure 5.11 to see that while there may be some truth to that claim, the trait variable is still very powerful, even having taken the fundamental variables into account. There we compare the effect of the traits on the vote when looking only at that variable and when taking the fundamentals into account. Notice also that it really doesn't matter whether we use the longer time span possible from the smaller set of fundamentals (party identification, ideology, and the three-issue scale) or the full set of fundamentals. Some portion of the original high power of the traits is due to their overlap with the fundamentals.

Further evidence of this is the fact that the correlation between the trait scale and the party identification scale has increased from .52 in 1980 to .80 in 2020 it is .80.[36] Consider also Figure 5.12. There we report the difference

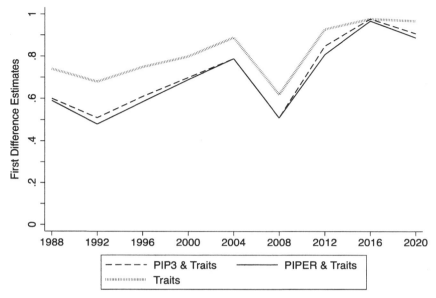

Figure 5.11. Fundamentals, traits, and presidential vote, first differences, 1988–2020

Note: Estimates derived by calculating the difference of predicted probabilities at the twenty-fifth and seventy-fifth percentile values of the candidate traits scale variable. Predicted probabilities are generated from logistic regression models regressing presidential vote choice on PIP3 and candidate trait variables or PIPER and candidate trait variables, or only candidate trait variables. Data point for 1996 PIPER & Traits is missing, and the line connects 1992 and 2000.

Source: Compiled by authors from the ANES Time Series Cumulative Data File, the 2000 ANES Time Series Study, and the 2016 ANES Time Series Study. Candidate trait variables for 2012 and 2020 obtained from the 2012 ANES Time Series Study and the 2020 ANES Time Series Study.

in trait evaluations of the two candidates by respondent partisanship. We see that these differences in evaluations have grown over time, especially among Democrats in 2012 and 2016 and for both partisans in 2020. That is, partisans see greater differences in the traits of the candidates over time, a sort of partisan polarization of evaluations of the candidates.

The various results suggest that the traits might better be thought of as "mediating" the role of the fundamentals. That is to say, the evaluations of the candidate traits stand in between the fundamentals and the vote. The fundamentals help explain how voters evaluate the candidates, and these evaluations then are some of the most important election-specific features that shape the vote. Partisanship, ideology, and the other forces, that is, act at least in part *through* the traits to shape the vote. This "acting through" is

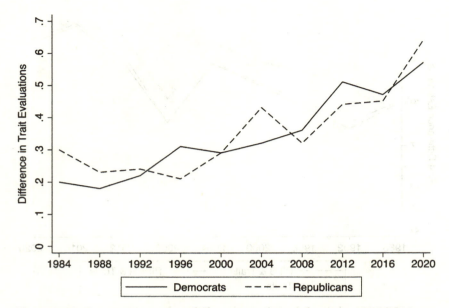

Figure 5.12. Increasing partisan differences in trait evaluations, 1984–2020

Note: Estimates derived from differences in the mean values of in-party and out-party candidate trait evaluation among Democrats and Republicans.

Source: Compiled by authors from the ANES Time Series Cumulative Data File, the 2000 ANES Time Series Study, and the 2016 ANES Time Series Study. Candidate trait variables for 2012 and 2020 obtained from the 2012 ANES Time Series Study and the 2020 ANES Time Series Study.

a "mediating effect," and it is just what the authors of *The American Voter* (1960) meant by long-term forces orienting the voter to electoral politics and helping shape the short-term forces that are more immediately related to the vote. In addition, this is just what Stokes (1966) sought to show about how candidate evaluations were the especially relevant short-term force for explaining electoral outcomes, above and beyond their relationship to the only then-relevant long-term force, partisanship. The differences today are that there are more fundamentals than in the 1950s and early 1960s and that these are increasingly closely related to each other and to the vote. If this is so, and if they are thereby increasingly important in orienting the voter to the election and its specific candidates, then we should observe a significant mediating role for the traits, and their role should be increasingly closely related to the fundamentals over the years.

Let us consider this possibility more closely. Figure 5.13 provides a path diagram of traits as a mediator, and Figure 5.14 presents the results of a

EVALUATIONS OF CANDIDATES AND CAMPAIGNS 111

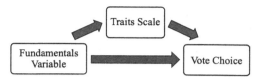

Figure 5.13. Path diagram of potential relationship
Source: Compiled by authors.

classic Baron and Kenny (1986) three-step mediation test, updated to the more contemporary procedures in Imai et al. (2010). A variable functions as a mediator when it meets the following conditions: (a) variations in levels of the independent variable (fundamentals) significantly account for variations in the presumed mediator (trait scale); and (b) variations in the mediator (trait scale) significantly account for variations in the dependent variable (vote choice), and (c) when both the main independent variable and the

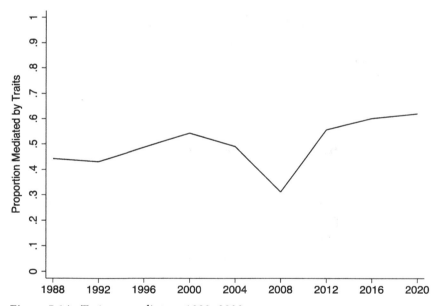

Figure 5.14. Traits as mediators, 1988–2020

Note: Estimates obtained from Baron and Kenny's (1986) mediation approach. The fundamentals variable and candidate traits variables reduced to their first principal component using PCA. Data point for 1996 is missing, and the line connects 1992 and 2000.

Source: Compiled by authors from the ANES Time Series Cumulative Data File, the 2000 ANES Time Series Study, and the 2016 ANES Time Series Study. Candidate trait variables for 2012 and 2020 obtained from the 2012 ANES Time Series Study and the 2020 ANES Time Series Study.

112   THE FUNDAMENTAL VOTER

mediator are included in one equation, the effect of the independent variable (fundamentals) on the dependent variable (vote choice) is zero. Partial mediation occurs when the effect of the independent variable on the dependent variables is weakened but not erased by the inclusion of the mediator variable.

The results presented in Figure 5.14 show that the trait scale variable does, in fact, partially mediate the relationship between the fundamentals and vote choice.[37] The proportion mediated captures the proportion of the effect of the fundamentals on vote choice that goes through the mediator, rather than through some other set of variables or directly from the fundamentals to the vote. The results show that the fundamentals account for variations in both vote choice and the trait scale. Including the trait scale variable as mediator shows from election to election that there is much stability in the effect of the traits as mediator of the fundamentals. That is, the trait scale is statistically significant and grows in strength as a mediator over the years, such that the proportion of the effect of the fundamentals that affects the vote is shaped to a slowly increasing degree to which it is more strongly affecting the traits, which in turn affects the vote. Thus, the traits' role as mediator increases from 44 percent in 1988 to 62 percent in 2020.[38] Indeed, unlike many other cases in this book in which changes over time have been gradual but consistent, the increase in mediation is relatively slight until 2008 and then increases rapidly.

The Fundamentals Shape Electoral Campaigns

In earlier chapters we found that the fundamental forces in electoral politics have grown in importance, such as in being closely related to voting choices. In Chapter 2 we found this was true individually, and in Chapter 4 we found this was true as an aggregate, as the fundamentals have become increasingly close to forming a single force that divides the electorate in ways that transform it from "merely" a set of long-term forces into a single, increasingly broad, and increasingly deep line of cleavage. In Chapter 3 we found, inter alia, that the fundamentals have led to increasing polarization in the electorate, but a unique type of polarization that is distinctly different from the growing extremism of partisan polarization among elected political leaders.

In this chapter we found that this increasingly strong approximation of a single line of cleavage operates much the way that party identification did in the 1950s and 1960s, when Stokes (1966) traced out party identification's role as the sole empirically relevant, long-term attitude shaping short-term and more proximate attitudes in the election. The key difference from then is that the growth to five fundamentals from one has meant that partisanship now is infused with a greater amount and variety of substantive politics—and as we see here, affective politics as well.

This cleavage of the electorate has changed congressional elections and thus helps us understand the transformations of elections that began in the 1980s. It appears to have changed how the electorate approaches learning about candidates, at least the presidential contenders at the start of the nomination campaigns. And it appears to be an increasingly important force in understanding the public's affective evaluations of the candidates (as measured through feeling thermometers) and of understanding—and coming to different views of—the traits of the presidential nominees. The fundamentals therefore operate just as Campbell et al. (1960) claimed long-term forces should: they help orient the public to elections and the parties, issues, and candidates that are contesting for office. The difference is that party identification is no longer the sole long-term force. It has been joined by a host of others, and each brings to the others different political content that has infused electoral politics now, unlike seventy years ago, and that has transformed electoral behavior since the mid-1980s.

Appendix to Chapter 5 Mediation Analysis

In reference to Figure 5.13 and Figure 5.1A, perfect mediation occurs when the effect of the fundamentals on the vote goes to zero in the presence of the trait scale. Partial mediation (as we find here) occurs when the direct effect of the fundamentals on the vote decreases significantly with inclusion of the traits (in the literature, just how much is enough to be nontrivial is unresolved). Our results are large enough to be self-evidently "significant," no matter where one stands in the debate.

We performed the analysis reported in Figure 5.14 and the text above using the mediation model presented in Imai et al. (2010), using the nonparametric bootstrapping method with one thousand resamples to compute the indirect effect of the mediator. We used the R-package provided by Tingley et al. (2020). The models in our analyses include the SES and demographic along with the fundamental variables. Those variables are included in the mediation model as the first principal component of the analysis of the PIPER variables.

The proportion mediated is calculated by dividing the average causal mediation effect (ACME) by the total effect, where the ACME is the estimate of the mediator on the dependent variable after controlling for the independent variable, and the total effect is

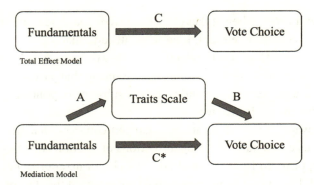

Figure 5.1A. Baron and Kenny's mediation approach

Note: C = the total effect of the fundamentals on vote choice; C = C* + AB where C* is the direct effect of the fundamentals on vote choice after controlling for the traits scale; C* = C – AB where AB is the indirect effect of the fundamentals on vote choice. Perfect mediation occurs when the effect of the fundaments on vote choice decreases to 0 with the traits scale in the model. Partial mediation occurs when the effect of the fundamentals on vote choice decreases by a nontrivial amount with the traits scale in the model (Baron and Kenny, 1986).

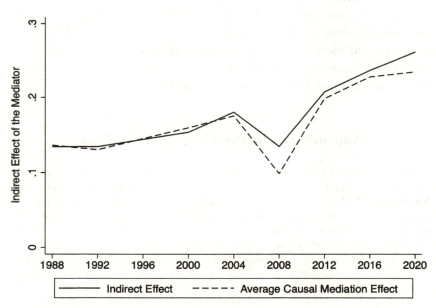

Figure 5.2A. Traits as mediators of fundamentals and presidential vote

Note: Lines show how traits mediate the fundamentals and the presidential vote using two ways of estimating the effect of the mediator. The indirect effect estimates are obtained from Baron and Kenny's (1986) mediation approach, and the average causal mediation effect estimates are obtained from Imai et al.'s (2010) causal mediation framework. Data points for 1996 are missing, and the lines connect 1992 and 2000.

Source: Compiled by authors from the ANES Time Series Cumulative Data File, the 2000 ANES Time Series Study, and the 2016 ANES Time Series Study. Candidate trait variables for 2012 and 2020 obtained from the 2012 ANES Time Series Study and the 2020 ANES Time Series Study.

the estimate of the independent variable on the dependent variable. In other words, the ACME is the estimate of the trait scale in the full regression model, and the total effect is the estimate of the fundamentals variable in the regression of the fundamentals on vote choice. The total effect could also be calculated by adding the estimates of ACME and the estimate of the independent variable in the full regression model that controls for the mediator.

In each year considered, conditions (a) and (b) in the following figures are met; that is, our fundamentals variable accounts for variations in both vote choice and the trait scale variable.

We also ran the more traditional Baron and Kenny analysis (1986). We report the comparison between the two in Figure 5.2A, where the reader can see they are very similar.

6

The Fundamentals

From Polarization to a Single Reinforced Cleavage

In Chapter 4 we examined how the five fundamentals have generated a particular kind of polarization in the electorate, one due primarily to sorting. That is to say, Democrats have become increasingly consistent in the sense of responding that they are liberal on ideology and in policy positions, relatively unresentful about race, and more positive about the past performance of the economy, when Democrats are in charge, than Independents and Republicans. Republicans, for their part, have become increasingly consistent on ideology, issues, racial resentment, and beliefs about economic performance as well, just on the other side of the divide. Another way to say this is that the fundamentals first grew in numbers (from one to five). They then became increasingly correlated with each other, and we showed earlier just how sharp the increase in correlation among the various pairs of fundamentals has become since the 1980s. In addition, the electorate as a whole is distributed on each fundamental in the 2020s pretty much as voters were in the 1970s. Increased sorting with only modestly changed distributions overall requires a great deal of change at the level of individual citizens to create the form of polarization found in the electorate. How might this electoral polarization have occurred?

How Elites Polarized by Party

We point to two major changes among political elites that at least support and may have launched the public's sorting. These changes clearly came first in time, long before voters changed, and in that sense at least (and quite possibly in more important senses), the elites led the voters to change in such a manner that the public "sorted" without becoming all that much more extreme on most concerns.

The Fundamental Voter. John H. Aldrich, Suhyen Bae, and Bailey K. Sanders, Oxford University Press.
© Oxford University Press 2024. DOI: 10.1093/oso/9780197745489.003.0006

One of the most important consequences of elite polarization was the ability to change policy in very important ways. The long run of Democratic dominance in the national government was paused during the Reagan years, but except for a very brief moment, the Republicans did not control the House and therefore could not really implement the full range of policy changes they desired.[1] It was not until after the 1994 congressional elections, when the forty-year run of Democratic House majorities finally ended, that the GOP was in a position to have a real (although still incomplete) impact on public policy.[2] While partisan polarization in Congress was well underway before then, the 1994 "Republican revolution" was much closer in time to the electoral sorting. And it was not until the George W. Bush administration that Republicans finally held unified control of government (from 2001 to 2007).

From the end of Reconstruction through the mid-1970s, southern Whites in the electorate were disproportionately Democratic, even though they were more conservative on ideology and many issues than their northern peers, and they were very often acting in support of the racially resentful. They were also generally less enthused about the macroeconomic consequences of having Democrats in Washington, especially in the 1950s and 1960s, when a major part of national Democratic economic policies was based on creating expensive social programs. One might well imagine that these southern Democrats and, perhaps even more, the citizens who supported them, "belonged" in the Republican Party. They might well have joined, were it feasible to do so.

The Jim Crow system of the South was justly infamous for excluding Blacks from voting and other aspects of political, economic, and social life.[3] But another key part of Jim Crow was to ensure that the Republican Party (or any other party except the White southern Democratic Party) could survive electorally in that region. Many general election contests featured one White Democrat and literally no one else. Other races had one effective and well-supported White Democrat and one or more ineffective and unsupported contenders, so that the Democrat received 75, 80, even 90 percent of the vote. As a result, White southern citizens, regardless of their political inclinations, registered as Democrats because their primary was the only place where they could make real and consequential political choices. Citizens registered with a party with which they disagreed at the national level, at least on some very important policies, in part so that they could vote in the only election that mattered in their state, the Democratic primary.[4]

118   THE FUNDAMENTAL VOTER

The Civil Rights and Voting Rights Acts and much of the rest of the Great Society and War on Poverty programs of the Lyndon B. Johnson administration began to change all that. As Johnson is alleged to have said at the time, "We have lost the South for a generation." Given that this was at the era of high levels of incumbency advantage, it took nearly that entire generation for electorally safe, incumbent, White, southern Democrats to age out of Congress. That process began in earnest in the 1980s and reached a final denouement in the 1994 congressional elections, in which the Republicans not only won the majority of the House seats for the first time in forty years but also won the majority of seats from the South for the first time since Reconstruction.

With this change, conservative southern Democrats in the electorate could finally find at least potentially competitive, conservative, southern Republican candidates to vote for, and one big piece of the sorting happened. They could finally become the Republicans they well might have been long before, if only it were possible. Note that it was not that the White conservatives in the southern electorate became more conservative; they could hold to more or less the same positions they had always held. It was just that they had an actual choice and could express their fundamental political views by choosing between two parties for the first time in their lives in ways that so many outside the South had always been able to do.

The second big shift was less dramatic and traumatic than needing to overthrow Jim Crow to give conservative White southerners their effective choice, but it was something of a counterbalancing shift of genuine significance. Opposition to slavery, the Confederacy, so-called Redemption, and the Jim Crow system had consistently come from the Northeast and especially New England. The Republican Party emerged in the North in the 1850s.[5] Republicans tended to win most elections in these areas, even after Franklin D. Roosevelt in the twentieth century won support from immigrants, union members, and blue-collar workers in general, in the cities of those states. The response to the turmoil in the South in the 1950s and 1960s was a Republican Party that agreed on conservative economic policies, but with an important wing of these states' Republican leadership supporting more liberal civil rights and other social issues. These were the so-called Rockefeller Republicans.[6] They were politically nearly the opposite of the White southern Democrats.

When the conservative wing gained support in the South, the socially more liberal, Rockefeller, wing was either defeated or left the party. For example, in a tight contest, Sen. Barry Goldwater (R-AZ) defeated Nelson A.

Rockefeller for the 1964 Republican nomination for president. His delegates booed and heckled Rockefeller at their convention. Goldwater had recently voted against the Civil Rights Act of 1964. His general election campaign featured the Republican Party's first "southern strategy," successfully appealing to southern voters, yielding him victories in five southern states, but he received electoral votes from nowhere else except his home state of Arizona. All of this helped push socially liberal Republicans in the North out of the party, one way or another, and, if not they did not defect, they earned the RINO label (Republicans In Name Only) for the first time in the contemporary era. As in the South, the northern shifts began in the first decades after World War II but took decades more to fully sort out; inevitably they did. Thus, the two parties had roughly equal and opposite reactions to each other, leading to more fully sorted and likely more extreme political elites. The sorting required aligning one's partisanship with ideology, issues, and race, not necessarily having to change, let alone become more extreme, regarding these matters.[7]

Finally, in this era some major issues were bipartisan. One of the first things Eisenhower did as president was to demonstrate a commitment to key provisions of the New Deal, such as social security. This helped set at least a relatively high floor of bipartisan agreement, even if Democrats typically wanted to increase such programs more than Republicans did. The St. Lawrence Seaway, and even more, the interstate highway system were key new initiatives of the federal government that Eisenhower led. His vice president, Nixon, when elected president in 1968, supported major initiatives on environmental issues (e.g., the Clean Air and Clean Water Acts) that were broadly popular among Democrats. There may have been intraparty disagreements on these, but that only further supports the idea that much of importance was not polarized between the party elites in these decades.

Perhaps the most important example of all is the "bipartisan consensus on foreign policy," which was particularly focused on bipartisan agreement that the United States was engaged in the Cold War with the USSR and needed to stand firm against the communist threat. This Cold War consensus lasted from shortly after the end of World War II at least until the height of the Vietnam War. All agreed that the United States was to lead the western portion of this bipolar world. The Republican Party overcame its long isolationist tradition to enter into the bipartisan consensus, and this lasted at least through end of the Reagan administration. (Reagan was famous for his challenge, "Mr. Gorbachev, tear down this wall!") As was true regarding

120   THE FUNDAMENTAL VOTER

bipartisan policies on the domestic side, there were intraparty divisions, first among the remaining isolationist Republicans (a position some Republican politicians appear to be adopting today) and then more deeply among Democrats over the Vietnam War. As on the domestic side, internal divisions only add to the case of these major issues not contributing to partisan polarization at the elite level—and no need for partisan sorting in the public.

All of this seems perfectly reasonable. Transforming the South at last into a truly competitive democracy led to an equal and opposite reaction among Republicans that presented the public with an increasingly fully sorted set of political elites, which combined with the breakdown of bipartisan agreements and the end of the Cold War to create the elite partisan distributions we see in the congressional polarization of today. When this pattern was seen by the electorate and they reacted by becoming much more fully sorted on a large number of fundamentals about politics, we were left with a picture of an electorate no longer lacking in issue and ideological choices and thus in issue-voting abilities, but even more, no longer as innocent about so much of politics. But perhaps, like all things that are carried on too long and pushed too far toward the extremes (at least as is happening at the elite level), even well-sorted parties can become problematic. And it is this process we explore in this chapter.

Growing Numbers of Fundamentals Become an Increasingly Strong Dimension

As we saw earlier, we are able to include all five fundamentals in our analyses by the mid-1980s. It was at just about that time that the correlation among party identification, ideology, and issues began to increase (the reader might refer back to Figure 4.9). These correlations were all quite low as late as 1988. They hovered around .3—certainly not zero, but hardly substantively strong for variables serving as fundamental forces in electoral politics. But that began to change such that by the Trump era, these correlations now were in the .6 range and by 2020 even higher, a magnitude that is much more substantial and meaningful. At the same time, we can also see that the ability of the public to satisfy the Campbell et al. (1960) conditions for understanding and potentially employing issues and ideology in reaching choices was increasing just as dramatically. Because the measures are incomplete in these earlier years, we cannot be certain about how economic retrospection and racial

FROM POLARIZATION TO A SINGLE CLEAVAGE   121

resentment would have fit into this account. Insofar as we can judge, however, they too fit the post-1980 patterns of party, ideology, and issues over time. As Figure 4.10 showed, including these two additional fundamentals lowered the average pair-wise correlations among the fundamentals somewhat but did not change the over-time pattern.

One of Poole and Rosenthal's core conclusions about roll-call voting in Congress is that it has become increasingly *unidimensional* in both House and Senate.[8] Many have suggested that polarization in the public means, if nothing else, an increasingly unique, single dimension for assessing politics. The evidence we have provided so far clearly suggests the inference that the public's views on fundamentals are increasingly unidimensional as well. But we can provide more and stronger evidence on this critical point.

How might we know if electoral politics, with its increasingly large number of fundamentals, is nonetheless following in the footsteps of Congress by converging toward a unidimensional standard of evaluation? To be sure, there are more fundamentals, and they seem richer in political substance (and likely in affect). Does this broader and deeper set of fundamentals also look increasingly like a single dimension?

One standard statistical answer to the question of dimensionality involves looking at the items' "principal components," as tested through principal components analysis (PCA). The full details of the PCA analysis are found in the online appendix, in which we report the results for the three-variable PIP3 measure from the 1972 through 2020 ANES surveys and the full, five-variable PIPER measure for the available years (1988, 1992, and 2000–2020). The conventional rule of thumb is that a component is sufficiently important if what is known as its "eigenvalue" is greater than 1.00. As can be seen in the appendix, the first component always has an eigenvalue that meets that standard, generally by a considerable margin, while no other component in any year does so. Quite often, the second component comes close to but never exceeds it. Thus, we would say that there is enough structure to consider the fundamentals as forming a scale, and that scale is best described as unidimensional.[9]

How good is the description of that scale as a single dimension? The relevant guide to judgment is reported in Figure 6.1. In that figure, we report the percentage of the variance of these variables that is "explained" by the first dimension.[10] There are two observations we can make. One is that the first component does a decent, if not overwhelming, job in accounting for the patterns among these variables from the beginning of our time series.[11]

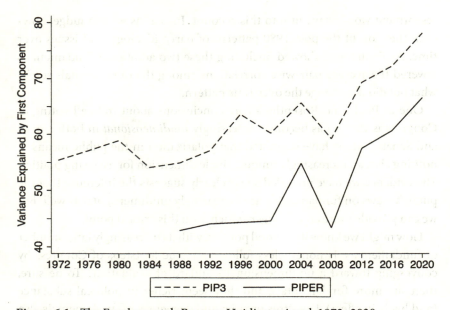

Figure 6.1. The Fundamentals Become Unidimensional, 1972–2020

Note: PIP3 and PIPER distributions obtained from first principal component scores from PCA analysis, standardized with mean centered at zero, and standard deviation is 1. Data point for 1996 PIPER is missing, and the line connects 1992 and 2000.

Source: Compiled by authors from the ANES Time Series Cumulative Study, the 2000 ANES Time Series Study, and the 2016 ANES Time Series Study.

The other is that we can thus answer this question in the affirmative, at least in the sense that there is clearly enough structure to say that it forms at least a one-dimensional scale, and we have no evidence that it forms more than one.

Our second question can be answered more affirmatively. The fundamentals have become increasingly unidimensional over time. The first component essentially doubles its minimal value over time, and this is true for both PIP3 and PIPER. Just as so many other measures and relationships we have studied have trended upward over time, so do the measures of unidimensionality of the fundamentals. That is to say, the first dimension has become a stronger account of these fundamentals, especially over recent elections. In the most recent elections, the strength of the first component hits the 70 percent mark for PIP3 and the 60 percent mark for PIPER. These data therefore reinforce (and are really just another aspect of) the increased correlation among these measures reported in earlier chapters.

That the fundamentals form a single dimension is perhaps consistent with Campbell et al. (1960) in their claim that only partisanship matters. Based on their 1950s data, they concluded that although other variables may be related to partisanship, they contribute little to the fundamentals scale. We consider therefore how these components of fundamentals relate to one another. One way to do so is to look at the "loadings" of the variables on the first component; that is to say, how important is each individual fundamental in composing that one dimension?[12] As the data in the appendix show, the first component in the PCA for PIP3 is an almost evenly balanced, three-way division among party, ideology, and issues. In no election year does one or even two variables play a leading role, and this three-way balance is reasonably constant over time. That is, even while their collective effect is growing over time, party, ideology, and issues are about evenly balanced in doing so. In the full set of five fundamentals (PIPER), the same three variables—party, ideology, and issues—are generally of similar size and generally are the three most heavily weighted variables. By about 2004, all five of the variables that make up the fundamentals are broadly similar in magnitude. Thus, we conclude with reasonable confidence that there is a single dimension and that this dimension is composed of party, ideology, and issues at roughly similar levels of importance, if not of all five fundamentals, and the strength of the single dimension appears to grow over time.[13]

There need be nothing wrong with a polarized political system. At one level, as we pointed out earlier, any vote with advocates on each side is polarized to some degree and along some line or another. Shortly after World War II, a committee of the American Political Science Association (1950) lamented the *absence* of polarization as inhibiting the full exercise of democratic politics in America.[14] What that committee called for was a "more responsible" party system, one in which the two parties offered clear and distinct alternatives to the public and stood by those differences upon gaining power. That is, they wanted a more polarized party system in the face of the intraparty divisions that muddled what it might mean to be a Democrat or a Republican, as we described in opening this chapter. By this century, they appear to have gotten what they proposed.

If, however, we can consider this single, well-sorted dimension to be a deep cleavage, then new and troublesome questions arise. The literature on cleavage politics tell us that this specific situation can become a threat to the stability of the democracy itself. We turn to this critical question to conclude our analysis.

124 THE FUNDAMENTAL VOTER

From Crosscutting to Reinforcing Cleavages among the Fundamentals

Throughout this book, we have described changes in electoral features as one or another kind of polarization. All of this is relatively benign, at least in principle, but also, at least in principle, there are very strongly negative possibilities that might arise with a single dimension. That is, too much of a good thing may become problematic.

We see three features as indicating that we may have reached a point where we have too much partisan polarization. First is the problem of extremism at the elite level. Assuming that the roll-call voting evidence really does indicate politicians in both parties moving toward their respective extremes, then abandoning the middle and offering mostly extreme proposals is inherently bad, probably so in all cases. But in a republican democracy, especially one with a mostly moderate public, it is certainly bad, describing a system that is distinctly unrepresentative of the public's preferences. Even at its best, one polarized party being in control of public policy means that at least a very large minority, and quite often an actual majority, of the public opposes the policies enacted by the party holding a congressional majority, no matter which party it is.[15] While divided government may lead to compromise, middle-of-the-road policies at least some of the time, as Mayhew (1991) argued, much has changed since he wrote—indeed, the great bulk of both congressional and electoral polarization has occurred since then. Moreover, this is not the only challenge our elites are posing to American democracy. Their expressions of negative affect have reached a point where the rhetoric of the most extreme politicians is threatening violence, rape, and even murder against their congressional peers and even their families. This is the problem of the depth of polarization in the fundamentals.

Second is that the increasing number, relevance, and electoral potency of the numbers of fundamentals means what was true in Congress since the 1980s remains true, and more so, today. This is not a case of "we are polarized in this way at one time, less polarized at another, and polarized in an entirely different way a third time." The long-term continuity of contemporary polarization, now approaching forty years or more, means there is no respite from unrepresentative party politics. This is the problem of breadth in terms of numbers of matters gathered together under polarization and in terms of its continuity over time.

The third feature is that it is not just the growing extremism of congressional roll call votes that is a problem.[16] It is not just the continuity of it. It is not even just the increasing breadth of polarization due to the spread of sorting across more and more-diverse fundamentals. It is all this, and finally, their combination of breadth and depth, combining all of them into a common basis of polarization. The growing unidimensionality that we have just shown indicates the possibility of an alarming growth of a single, broad and deep, increasingly heavily reinforced cleavage in American politics at both mass and elite levels.

Characterizing the political, social, and economic features of society as being composed primarily of crosscutting cleavages or of a mostly reinforcing one has long been a central concern of those who study democratic stability and durability. Let us consider what these stakes are, which we will see were laid out at the very founding of the American republic. Then we will turn to the evidence to make the final case that we are nearing the range at which the single reinforced cleavage poses serious risks to the stability of democracy in America.

Cleavages and the Stability of Democratic Institutions

James Madison made perhaps the single most important justification for the new Constitution in *Federalist* No. 10 (1961).[17] He argued that a principal justification for the expansion of the powers of the federal government from what they were under the Articles of Confederation was precisely the increase in the scope of society and government by expansion from mostly state-led politics under the Articles to the nation as a whole under the new Constitution. Expanding the scope generated increased numbers of interests, which in turn defined more—and more distinct—cleavages. Furthermore, as those numbers increased, he argued, it would become increasingly difficult for the new federal government to create and sustain a majority sufficient to take away the rights of citizens or adopt policies adverse to the permanent and aggregate interests of the society (as Madison defined tyranny). In short, it would be rare for a government in an extended republic to suffer from tyranny of the majority. The cause of the Revolution, he observed, was the gathering of too much power by the British government, enabling it to rule tyrannically over its unrepresented subjects in the American colonies. In the new democracy, we did not have to worry about the powers of a monarch.

126   THE FUNDAMENTAL VOTER

We did, however, have to worry about too much and too effective a set of powers in the government, even if elected by the public.

Madison imaged tyrannies both from majorities and from minorities. Democratic elections themselves were the most important solution to tyranny by a governing minority.[18] Majority tyranny, however, was different. Majority voting could not be counted on to take powers from a tyrannical government; that was how the tyrant gained power in the first place. Madison argued that expanding the scope of the nation increased the number and diversity of interests held throughout the public. As such, it would be increasingly difficult to attain tyrannical majorities in the first place and to maintain them in the second place. Too many of the special interests and concerns would crosscut other special interests and concerns, such that even if a majority formed, it would be hard to keep it together. Thus, crosscutting cleavages would reduce the possibility both of attaining and of maintaining majority tyranny.

It is at this point that the threat of a single cleavage comes in. A single, strong, broad, and deep cleavage would undermine that argument and, in its place, reintroduce the possibility of sustained majority tyranny. This, of course, was the problem of slavery that was so long, so broad, and so deep a reinforced cleavage that it required a Civil War and amendments to the Constitution even begin to overcome. It was impossible, in this case, to forge a sufficiently durable anti-slavery majority, amid America's intermingled but separated powers, to overcome a deeply entrenched electoral majority in the South (and elsewhere) that favored perpetuation of slavery. At least in the South, so many social and economic considerations were subsumed under the perpetuation of slavery and its related politics that the South was well understood as having a single, deep cleavage. In the North, there were of course interests generated from the benefits of slavery that flowed to northerners, but even ignoring them, the North was more Madisonian in being unable to forge a strong enough majority to disrupt the racially cleaved South. Indeed, southerners could break off legislators from the North to support them in Congress, leading to continual support for the institution, or at least to failure to end slavery in the antebellum period.

Today's circumstances are rather different. America as a whole has neared if not actually reached a point with a single cleavage, with apparently increasingly extreme elected officials and a well-sorted voting public. While not so extreme as those whom they elect, the public are also deeply divided into two camps. At this point, the two are quite close in size to each other, and only a few are not aligned with one or the other. The equal size of the two camps is what keeps one or the other side from winning most elections—from becoming a durable majority. If one side were to gain in relative size, that would translate into a durable majority, and Madison's threat of majority tyranny becomes likely.

The United States faced a similar situation at the end of Reconstruction. The reentry of former Confederates was completed by the end of Reconstruction, following the 1876 election. The consequent withdrawal of federal troops from the South made southern "redemption" possible. The return of White southerners to power, indeed to dominating power, in their states in turn led to a nation balanced between two parties. In national elections, Electoral College and House majorities swung from one party to the other in succeeding elections for twenty years. But then, in 1896, the great economic panic (inter alia) gave the Republicans a small but sustainable working majority in national politics (Brady 1973, 1988). This introduced a Republican era that lasted from 1896 until the Great Depression, with Republicans winning most national elections except when they were internally divided. This was sustainable because the Republican electoral majority in the North was balanced by the White southern Democratic Party dominance in the Jim Crow South. There, it effectively suspended democracy, driving virtually all Blacks and many poor White southerners out of the electorate until the 1960s, and also effectively banishing the Republican Party and, indeed any third party, from competition in nearly every district of the South.[19] Thus the Democratic Party essentially conceded the North and the national government to Republicans in exchange for being able to keep an uncompetitive, solid White Democratic South. As in slavery, under this Jim Crow system, southern Blacks (and some argue, northern Blacks as well) were a minority tyrannized over by a White majority. With this example, imagine what might happen, then, if one party or the other were to gain even a modest but persistent advantage on the one, singular cleavage?

We have noted Madison's philosophical account and substantive examples of extended majority tyranny in the United States. Let's consider the logic of that argument more carefully. Nicholas R. Miller (1983) provided a formal (i.e., mathematical) argument to support these claims. The great economist Kenneth J. Arrow (1963) had proved what he called the general possibility theorem in 1951. Arrow showed that, even if every person had clear, well-formed preferences, indicating that they knew well what they wanted the government to do, no one could possibly know for sure what the majority

128   THE FUNDAMENTAL VOTER

of citizens wanted the government to do. That is, well-formed preferences for individuals cannot always lead to well-formed goals for the government, supported by a majority. In this formal way, it appeared that logic supported the Madisonian account of multiple crosscutting interests leading to no durable majority. This meant that there was no logical or normative justification for any extended majority or its actions in government. For decades thereafter, social scientists and political philosophers struggled to get around Arrow's conclusion: there must be some way to elicit preferences from the public such that one could understand what the majority wanted. Otherwise, what meaning was there to elections?

Miller turned that concern on its head, quite as Madison had done. He argued that it was precisely because there was no normatively defensible way to form a majority preference that majority tyranny could not long endure. Every winner in a voting system could be defeated by some other, and therefore it was only a matter of time until even a tyrannical incumbent would be defeated. And there is good reason to believe the current majority will be overthrown rather quickly, at least under free and fair elections. When a party loses an election, it is incentivized to figure out how to defeat the erstwhile victors in the next election. That was, of course, Madison's point.

Our point is that if all the diverse crosscutting cleavages give way such that they all point in the same direction—that is, they each reinforce one another—then all the advantages of extending Madison's sphere are put to the side. There were no sufficiently strong competing interests to undermine the preference of a majority of White southerners for slavery in the South. It was economically, socially, and politically useful to keep slavery. That is economics, social structures, and politics all together pointed in the same direction.

Anglo-American and European nations democratized, at the fastest pace in the late nineteenth and early twentieth centuries. We are thereby able to observe that there are many different forms a government can take that we would all consider democratic. One of these forms is like America's, featuring a two-party system. In two-party systems, it is obvious, by definition, that one of the parties will get at least a few more votes than the other and thus win by a majority. But that is only by definition. Other democratic forms, such as those found in many countries on the European continent, have parliaments with multiparty systems. Many of these, for example, had party systems that tended to coalesce around generally Christian-liberal parties, while other parties tended to cluster on the left, around working-class, union, and social democratic parties.[20] But not all were defined by this more or less strictly left-right continuum. Other cleavages, over religion, ethnicity, language, urban-rural divides, and more, shaped party systems. The structure of political competition, even conflict, in any given nation, scholars argued, was related to the nature and extent of how much these various cleavages crosscut or reinforced one another. Too many crosscutting cleavages meant that parliamentary systems, in particular, had great difficulty forming a majority at all, quite like the fears of the first wave of scholarship about Arrow's theorem. Certainly, these scholars argued, there is too little basis for forming a majority coalition in parliament at all.[21] Alternatively, if one forms, it cannot sustain itself.[22] In either case, surely the foundations of democracy itself are challenged. Conversely, if the same party or coalition holds power without serious challenge, due to a single reinforced cleavage defining the politics of elections, then the minority that never gains access to power will become increasingly discouraged, perhaps sufficiently so to take action against the durable majority coalition. The consequence is that a lack of sufficient crosscutting cleavages will threaten the stability of the democratic order.

It thus appears that the degree of "crosscuttingness" (or its near-negative, the degree of "reinforcing-ness") of its cleavages is a critical feature of the stability of democratic politics. To quote from Rae and Taylor (1970, 13), "This may be illustrated by examining the oft-repeated hypothesis that cross-cutting cleavages conduce to lasting democratic political organization, whereas reinforcing systems of cleavage tend to undermine it." They then cite such authors as Truman (1951) and Lijphart (1968) and political philosophers such as Aristotle and John Stuart Mill, along with other social scientists, to buttress these points. Rae and Taylor summarize this work in their first proposition:

> Proposition 1: If there is not sufficient cross-cutting between politically relevant cleavages, then democratic political organization is not likely to be stable (1970, 106).

Rae and Taylor then turn to three more propositions. These are, in effect, summarized in the last of these propositions (their proposition 4), in which they say that if a society is "either too homogenous or too heterogeneous over racial, linguistic, and religious cleavages, then democratic political organization is not likely to be stable" (108). The cleavages of fundamentals we are about to study are not solely racial, linguistic, or religious, although they are related to these aspects.

130 THE FUNDAMENTAL VOTER

Measuring Crosscutting Cleavages

We now develop measures of crosscutting cleavages in American politics following Rae and Taylor. Like all good scientific work, theirs begins with definitions of key concepts and basic premises. It concludes by deducing propositions, in this case leading to their central propositions, 1 and 4 above.

Rae and Taylor define cleavages as follows. They begin by stating that "cleavages are the criteria which divide members of a community or subcommunity into groups, and the relevant cleavages are those which divide members into groups with important political differences at specific times and places" (1970, 1). They note that there are different kinds of cleavages as understood in the relevant literature. *Trait* cleavages are such ascriptive characteristics as race or caste. *Opinion* cleavages are exemplified as those defined by ideology or preference. Behavioral or *act* cleavages are those defined by voting or organizational membership. What is interesting is that Rae and Taylor's proposition 1 applies to all three of their types of cleavages. We are interested in the combination of all three. To be sure, our fundamentals are best described as attitudinal type cleavages, but their position in the very center of trait, attitudinal, and behavioral complexes suggests that they might also be taken to stand as measures directly or just slightly indirectly tapping all three.[23]

The cleavage structure of a society (or in their words, a "community") has three components (1970, 3). *Crystallization* indicates what proportion of the community is committed to any particular group centered in a cleavage.[24] *Fragmentation* asks how many members of the community find themselves in opposition to one another. Finally, the *intensity* of fragmentation indicates the strength of that opposition given by the cleavage. Rae and Taylor's theoretical and measurement strategies are thus based on the concatenation of these three components.

The key question raised in the electoral data is how individual positions on one cleavage are related to positions on another cleavage. We will study this more directly below, but it already appears in our data that in the 1970s there was a fairly high degree of crosscutting-ness in the cleavage structure. That is, the structure was of a numerous set of divisions into groups that were only weakly related to one another. While most citizens in those days found themselves opposing a group on one fundamental, very few opposed those others on many or all of them. But the growing reinforcement of the cleavage structure led to fewer and fewer distinct and weakly related groups. Rather,

FROM POLARIZATION TO A SINGLE CLEAVAGE   131

each line of cleavage tended increasingly to divide the electorate along nearly the same line, and thus the number of different and distinguishable groups shrank, more or less, to just two.

Measuring Cleavages with the Fundamentals

The questions that make up our measures of the five fundamentals are survey questions and therefore tend to the more continuous (or at least potentially ordinal) levels of measurement, rather than tapping the cleavage-defining nominal groups directly. Underlying our measures are those nominal categories, although transforming ordinal into nominal group data will leave us with a few choices to make. Let us start with the groups that make up the party cleavage. The seven-point party identification scale was long thought to be ordinal, running from least Republican (i.e., "strong Democrat") to most. More extended assessment showed that there are likely violations of the expected ordinality. In particular, those responding as party leaners tend to behave more like strong partisans and certainly more so than "weak" partisans. We take this as evidence that, at the very least, leaners should be treated as belonging to party groups (for more details, see Keith et al. 1992). Thus, we have three groups for the partisan cleavage; Democrats (strong, less strong, and leaning), Republicans (the comparable three responses), and Independents (the "pure" Independent response category). With so few third-party identifiers, we include them along with the group the ANES team consider "apolitical" and those who refused or were unable to answer the relevant questions as "not crystallized."

Ideology and issues are measured directly by handing respondents a card (or doing the online equivalent) with a seven-point scale on it. The ideology scale includes specific responses to all seven categories. Responses 1, 2, and 3 (5, 6, and 7) include the term "liberal" ("conservative"), and (akin to partisanship) we consider responses 1–3 as denoting being a liberal, 5–7 as being a conservative, and 4 as a third group (moderates or those who choose to be neither liberal nor conservative). Those who did not pick any of the seven points to indicate how they think of themselves in these terms are considered to be not crystallized. Our PIP3 and PIPER five-issue scales are treated similarly.[25] To sum the three or five issues included in our scale, we count the number of "liberal" groups and "conservative" groups the citizen's responses indicate they chose. For the three-issue scale, a respondent is considered on

132 THE FUNDAMENTAL VOTER

the left (right) if they chose at least two of the issues, and if only two, they selected the moderate (4) response on the other scale.[26] For the five-scale measure, this takes at least three liberal (conservative) responses and up to two moderate responses. Any respondent who picks at least one liberal side and at least one conservative side is considered not to be either a liberal or a conservative and is included along with those who picked only 4 or only moderate responses throughout. Economic retrospection is divided into two groups, those who think the economy is getting better and those who think it is worse. Responding "better" to a Democratic incumbent supports that party's nominees and so is considered Democrat, "worse" is considered a Republican-supporting response, and the opposite applies if a Republican is the incumbent. Finally, racial resentment is divided in a similar fashion. Failure to give a substantive response to the question indicates noncrystallization.

Thus, we have definitions and measures of the nominal groups that make up the cleavage structure on each of the five fundamentals. Crystallization includes not being counted as having given a noncrystallized response, but that is a minimal definition, and we will look into that matter further. The next theoretically relevant variable is fragmentation. This is defined as the chances that two individuals are in the same group on any specific cleavage compared to being from a different pair of groups on that cleavage. We have assessed the distribution of responses to each of the fundamentals over the various elections already, but will do so even more directly soon. Most of our fundamentals have roughly equal numbers of citizens in the two main substantive groupings (Democrat-Republican, liberal-conservative, etc.), varying mostly in how large the middle group is. Independents are a fairly small proportion of crystallized citizens on the partisanship cleavage (8–12 percent). As we have seen, moderate, or point 4, responses are often modal on the seven-point issue and ideology scales, and the degree of noncrystallization especially in the early years was a major part of why Campbell et al. (1960) did not include either as a fundamental force in electoral politics.

Decline in the Extent of Crosscutting Cleavages

In this section we report on two measures. One is the direct translation of fragmentation into what we have called sorting. That is, just how many citizens are consistently Democratic/ideologically liberal/liberal on issues, are consistently Republican/ideologically conservative/conservative on issues, and are mixtures of both or consistently moderate, leaning in neither direction? That is essentially a measure of the changing nature of fragmentation on the fundamentals. The second measure is then to turn directly to Rae and Taylor's measure of crosscutting-ness of the cleavages.

Figure 6.2 reports on the percentages of citizens estimated to be consistently sorted into the liberal camp; those consistently sorted into the conservative camp; and those who are a mixture of liberal, conservative, and moderate, using the PIP3 measure. Doing so allows for continuous coverage of changes from 1972 through 2020. We find that Republicans "sort" consistently from the mid-1980s on. The Democrats, conversely, sort more recently, particularly following the Obama administration. By 2020, the two parties are equally sorted, both reaching approximately 25 percent and thus totaling a bit over a majority of the electorate.

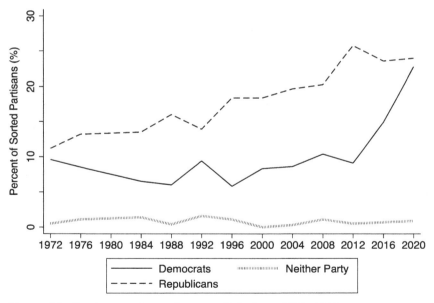

Figure 6.2. Partisan sorting on issues and ideology, 1972–2020

Note: "Neither party" includes those categorized as "pure" independents in the ANES, who score "4" on ideology and "0" on issues (with a score of –1 for a liberal and +1 for a conservative response). Data point for 1980 is missing, and the line connects 1976 and 1984.

Source: Compiled by authors from the ANES Time Series Cumulative Study, the 2000 ANES Time Series Study, and the 2016 ANES Time Series Study.

134 THE FUNDAMENTAL VOTER

Rae and Taylor developed their measure of crosscutting-ness (see also Taylor and Rae 1969) based on theoretical principles, with the idea being that a more theoretically derived measure is more useful when it comes to testing theories of politics that find the cleavage structure to be consequential. For the present, we look at the changes in their crosscutting measure over time. Their measure is structured such that the lower the number, the more the cleavages are reinforcing. Their measure varies between 0 and 1. A score of zero crosscutting-ness means that the two variables are not crosscutting at all and therefore would be fully reinforcing. For example, it will be zero for partisanship and ideology if all Republicans are conservatives and all Democrats are liberals. While there is a theoretical maximum of 1 if the crosscutting is complete, the actual maximum in any given data set depends in part upon the distribution of the two variables themselves (specifically, what Rae and Taylor call the degree of fragmentation). Realistically, this empirical maximum can be no lower than 0.5, but its achievable maximum is often somewhere between 0.5 and 1.0. Given, however, that the means and variances of our individual measures are relatively constant over time, we can compare crosscutting-ness over time because the achievable maximum crosscutting-ness is unlikely to have changed appreciably. We report these measures for the three pairs of variables in PIP3 because they cover the longest time span. We also report all of the pair-wise crosscutting measures between party and the remaining variables in the fuller set of PIPER for the available years.

As Figure 6.3 demonstrates, each of our three variable pairings traces essentially continuous declines. These begin to be noticeable in the 1980s, turn more sharply downward around 2000, and decline more precipitously thereafter, with the largest decline coming between 2016 and 2020. Starting at rather high levels of crosscuttingness, the declines in this measure—which is to say the increase in reinforcing-ness—have reduced substantially, perhaps especially the party-issues air. Thus, party, ideology, and issues have become consistently more reinforcing of one another, election after election.[27]

Earlier we illustrated how the electoral form of polarization differed from that of partisan polarization in Congress by reporting how the distribution of responses to each of the fundamentals was not the bipolar-empty-center shape found in Congress. Rather, the electorate has shown no more than a modest increase in the number of those with more extreme preferences on a fundamental. Instead, the electorate remains mostly moderate or at least near to that center on one fundamental after the other.

FROM POLARIZATION TO A SINGLE CLEAVAGE   135

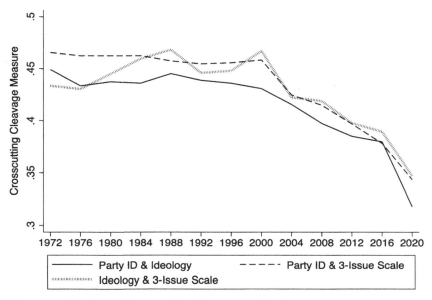

Figure 6.3. Decline of crosscutting cleavages, 1972–2020

Note: Data points for 1980 Party ID & 3 Issue Scale and Ideology & 3 Issue Scale are missing, and the lines connect 1976 and 1984.

Source: Compiled by authors from the ANES Time Series Cumulative Study, the 2000 ANES Time Series Study, and the 2016 ANES Time Series Study.

We can now see whether this mostly moderate version of electoral polarization holds true in the full combination of the fundamentals—our best indicator of the nature of the reinforced cleavage. We have shown earlier in this chapter that the fundamentals have become increasingly reinforcing of each other. It could be, of course, that a voter always being on the same side instead of sometimes on one side and sometimes on the other means that that voter ends up being more extreme (something we found to be true for the electorate overall). As Figure 6.4 clearly demonstrates, that is just not the case. While there is a bit broader spread, the distribution of the public on the combined PIP3 measure is a bit broader; most voters are clustered near the center; and it stands in stark contrast to congressional polarization, which is sharply and increasingly bipolar, with a clear demonstration of the absence of a congressional center. We show this for selected years, comparing congressional and PIP3-electoral polarization, but in the online appendix we show this is true year after year and whether one uses PIP3 or PIPER. Thus, we conclude that the electorate has polarized along the lines of "sorting"

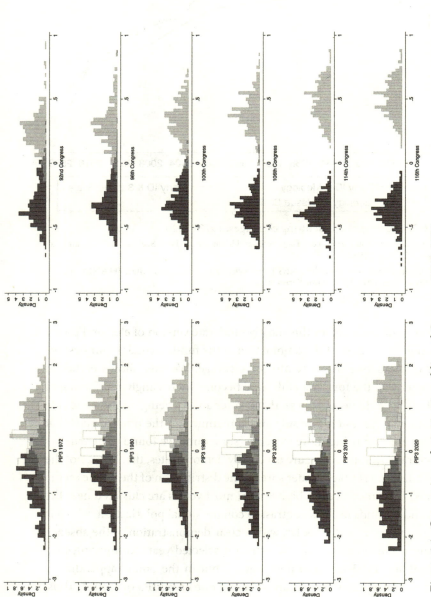

Figure 6.4. Comparing polarization in public and Congress, 1972–2020

Note: Histogram of PIP3 distribution in the public and congressional members' ideology by partisanship, with dark gray representing Democrats, light gray representing Republicans, and white representing Independents. PIP3 distribution obtained from first principal component scores from PCA analysis standardized with mean centered at zero and standard deviation is 1.

Source: Compiled by authors from the ANES Time Series Cumulative Study, the 2000 ANES Time Series Study, and the 2016 ANES Time Series Study. Polarization in Congress measured with DW-NOMINATE scores from Lewis et al., *Voteview: Congressional Roll-Call Votes Database,* 2023, https://voteview.com.

and not along the lines of clustering more strongly toward the extreme as in Congress. It is clear that by this measure at least, the electorate differs dramatically from the Congress they elect.

In sum, we believe that the evidence points to the fundamentals having an increasingly strong and coherent internal structure. Moreover, no single fundamental is more important than the others in defining that internal structure, such that it is a reasonable approximation to weigh each fundamental equally. Finally, the evidence is clear that, especially since about 1984, these fundamentals have increasingly reinforced one another in both the technical and conventional senses of that term. There is now a cleavage within the fundamentals that determine how voters orient themselves toward politics.

7

Conclusion

We began our study of the transformation of electoral politics by observing that both congressional and presidential elections before 1984 looked much different from those that followed. In seeking to understand why national elections changed so dramatically, we learned that it was not just elections but the very nature of democratic politics that changed. The first observable difference was the growth of congressional partisan polarization. In 1952, when national election surveys began to give us a rich picture of the voting public, partisan polarization in Congress (and we suspect elsewhere among political elites) was at a century-long historical low. What we came to see was that a series of crosscutting cleavages reduced polarization not only in Congress but presumably also among the public to its lowest point.

The civil rights movement and the federal government finally overcame congressional obstacles and were able to end the Jim Crow system in the South. The eventual consequences were the development of two-party politics in that region and then, ultimately, the conversion of many political elites and then much of the public in the South to the Republican Party. This set in motion countervailing changes among Republicans in the North. Congressional politics began to reflect this more sorted partisan politics, with the beginnings of undermining White southern Democratic control of Congress in the 1970s (see Rohde 1991; Aldrich 2011), the rise of Republicans to control the presidency and Senate in the 1980s, and the conversion of the South to a Republican majority in the electorate at nearly the same time that the Republicans took control of the House in the 1990s. The new Republican House majority, of whom most were from the South, began to make more negative speeches and take more negative actions. We suspect that this either set in motion or at least reflected the beginnings of the movement of each party toward its extreme ideological pole. That is, the change from a partisan sorting of the House to a partisan polarizing of the House (and at about the same time, the Senate) happened when Republicans were able to contest Democrats regularly for control of the House—and the Senate, and the presidency. A coherent cleavage with a truly competitive

The Fundamental Voter. John H. Aldrich, Suhyen Bae, and Bailey K. Sanders, Oxford University Press.
© Oxford University Press 2024. DOI: 10.1093/oso/9780197745489.003.0007

contest to be the governing majority induced an increasingly negative emotional response from the political elites in the 1990s, a trend that has only accelerated through the present.

The public responded to this increasing elite polarization, as we saw, by first observing it with reasonable accuracy as it happened and then beginning to adjust their views to the new political world they were observing. We demonstrated that the public began to develop attitudes and beliefs that helped them orient themselves to this new electoral world. A first measure was the growth in the number of citizens able to employ ideology and recurring issues, that is, the first signs of a growing level of political substance to the fundamental forces that helped them achieve this orientation. We cannot be sure when racial beliefs and economic evaluations became comparably fundamental, given that our measures did not regularly appear until the 1980s, but we suspect these were important fundamentals well before then. As these fundamentals increased in breadth and depth, partisanship itself went from being a relatively insubstantial political orientation, important though it was, to one associated with considerable political substance through its increasing association with the other fundamentals.

This pattern provides, we believe, the explanation for how and why national elections changed in the 1980s through the 2020s. We have shown how these fundamentals have become increasingly strongly related to congressional and presidential votes. These fundamentals, that is, have been fulfilling their role of orienting the public to electoral politics to an ever-increasing degree. Indeed, by 2020 their success in orienting the electorate was overwhelming. Knowing where a voter stood on the fundamentals in 2020 will lead us to correctly understand how seventeen of twenty voters voted for Congress and how nineteen of twenty voted for president. Short-term attitudes could matter, but they could not deflect overwhelming majorities from voting in the direction toward which their position on the fundamental forces oriented them.

The key to all this is the sorting of the electorate across the various fundamentals. The public's orientation to politics is revealed by the aligning of each of the fundamentals, so that they pointed voters in the same direction. While voters find themselves often, increasingly nearly always, on the same side as their party, even more important is their believing that the opposition is wrong on nearly everything of electoral importance. While increasingly many voters are on the same side as their partisans in office, this does not mean that they are close to them in all matters. So far (and we recognize this

140   THE FUNDAMENTAL VOTER

could be changing), voters have not deviated very far from being a "mostly moderate" electorate, unlike those whom they elect. They might vote for their more extreme partisan officeholders but need not feel any more warmly about them. But they can look at the opposition and say that their opposition partisans in the electorate are wrong on almost everything; indeed, it is the opposition candidates and officeholders who are viewed as increasingly far removed from them and thereby increasingly wrong. The result is a growing sense of antipathy toward opposing partisans.

In Chapter 5 we looked especially at the presidential candidates and at measures of how the public feels about them. As we noted, the candidates have long been a central component of the short-term attitudes that stand between the fundamentals and the vote, and it is the candidates in particularly who add the dynamism to elections. This dynamism seems to be receding as the fundamentals have a greater and greater influence over those short-term attitudes and how the public votes. Elections bounce around much less than they used to, and incumbents are less advantaged individually. We did not develop a full accounting of all short-term attitudes, to be sure. We focused on the candidates because of the role they play in generating electoral dynamism. And of all the possible aspects of candidates one might consider, we focused particularly on the affective, emotional measures of candidates. This allowed us to consider just how much voters' emotional responses could be attributed to the growing coherence of the fundamentals and the political substance they (at least in part) represent. We do not claim that we have a clear and statistically defensible measure of fundamentals *causing* affective evaluations by the candidates and parties.[1] But we believe that understanding the sorting induced among the fundamentals allows us to consider the growing importance of the most negative responses to politics not just as reflecting pure affect but as a complex intertwining of political substance *and* emotion. Affective partisanship appears to us to be not just "tribalism" but also deep disagreement about the directions that politics and policy should take in America.

In Chapter 6 we returned to political philosophy and to a broader comparison among democracies to consider the potential consequences of this broad, deep, increasingly singular cleavage. The short answer was that a politics driven by such a cleavage risks not just the stability of any given majority, day to day, but also the stability of the democracy itself. At the moment we are spared the worst consequence, what happens when one side or the other secures a durable working majority. At that point the proposition that

CONCLUSION 141

a single cleavage threatens democratic stability would be put directly to the test. But we can make two observations. One is that recent years have seen the degree of crosscutting cleavages that Madison so valued rapidly collapse. The second is how hard both parties are working to shape an electorate that gives them even a small working margin—and the fear they evince of the consequences should the other side succeed.

We do not have a simple formula to solve this problem. History does teach us two lessons in this regard, however. The first is that the risk of democratic backsliding arises when one side is able to embed its coalition in the institutions of democracy. The exemplar case is the Jim Crow South. Southern states succeeded in writing extensive legislation (and used extra-legal violence) to ensure that what was, in their case, a minority of the citizenry could nearly always win every election. This tyrannical electoral (even if not preference-based) majority lasted for generations and required mass movements, Supreme Court decisions, and federal laws working together to unwind it in order to create an actual multiparty, competitive democracy in the South.

Conversely, history also shows us that no matter how deeply a majority may be embedded, the truism that majorities are hard to attain but harder to maintain also holds. This was theoretically the point of Madison (and Arrow, Miller, and Riker). Just as the Democratic Party was creating the Jim Crow system in the South, the Republican Party secured a small but sustainable majority in the nation as a whole. Prairie Radicals and other western Progressives became a part of the Republican Party in part in rejection of the Populists' alignment with the southern-based Democratic Party in the 1890s. By 1910 these younger, more radical Republicans were chafing under the hold of the more traditional Republicans, leading to the revolt against Speaker Joseph G. Cannon in 1910 and the division between President William Howard Taft, representing the old guard, and former President Theodore Roosevelt, who bolted from the party after losing its nomination in 1912 and ran a third-party, "Bull Moose" or Progressive Party campaign. This enabled the Democrats to win and hold office through World War I.

The Great Depression ended the Republicans' majority and led to the New Deal Democratic majority. But divisions soon formed in that majority as well. By the late 1930s southern Democrats in Congress organized to serve as a balancer holding power over the minority Republicans and the (usually) minority of northern Democrats. Southern Democrats effectively determined which majority would prevail, whether it was the vote of the Democratic majority or that of a Conservative Coalition majority formed on the floor of Congress. They held the balance of power over federal policymaking because of the unresolvable divisions between them and their northern Democratic peers.

Both parties have held majorities in Congress in recent years. But although the parties are now clearly distinct from each other, majority power doesn't necessarily lead to the implementation of a cohesive policy agenda. Both parties feature considerable ideological diversity within their ranks, if not, on the Republican side, racial diversity. For instance, 2010 witnessed a surge in the public called the Tea Party, whose members eventually aligned primarily with the Republicans. In office, they differed from their non–Tea Party fellow partisans in distinct ways. Soon the Freedom Caucus formed in the Republican House, which eventually led to the ouster of one speaker, an early retirement of a second one, and the ouster of a third. The Democratic majority, for its part, is split between the progressive wing and the more moderate Democrats, something Sen. Bernie Sanders (I/D-VT) looked to capitalize on in the 2016 and 2020 presidential nomination campaigns. Thus, even with a deeply divided Congress and electorate, there remains great diversity within each of those relatively homogenous political parties, giving continuing relevance to the aphorism that majorities are hard to maintain. There is no guarantee that one party won't capture such strong support among the public that it can tyrannize over a minority party and its supporters in the electorate. We do not hope for an event as cataclysmic as the Depression to be the single point of destruction of a substantial electoral majority, but we do believe that there are so many interests of such differing kinds that it is very likely that any majority will be beset by internal and external disagreements and preferences, attitudes, beliefs, and interests that keep even as deep and strong a cleavage as we observe today from holding together over the long haul. We need only ensure that a smaller even more cohesive minority cannot take control long enough to pass laws that, as in Jim Crow, ensure a majority who oppose them cannot form in elections. If this can be accomplished, then we expect that the richness and diversity of the American public will eventually ensure that neither side is able long to tyrannize over the other.

Notes

Chapter 1

1. We examine elections to the US House and to the presidency in this book because these are the two elections with contests throughout the nation.
2. A correlation is a measure of how two variables move together. It runs from a minimum of −1 to a maximum of +1. A correlation of zero means the two variables are independent of each other; that is, how one changes has no relationship to how the other one does. A positive number means that as one variable increases, so does the other, with a negative indicating that when one increases, the other decreases.
3. It is not a coincidence that O'Neill served as a member of Congress from 1953 to 1987, essentially bracketing the era of incumbency advantage.
4. We would like to thank to Gary Jacobson and Jamie Carson for sharing their data; see Jacobson and Carson per comm February 7, 2022.
5. It is not just that incumbency implies easy re-election. In 1976 and 1980 incumbency was arguably critically important, but because the incumbents were unpopular, they suffered a close electoral defeat in 1976 and an even more one-sided defeat of the incumbent in 1980.
6. This was due in no small part to "Reagan Democrats," often those elected from the South at 45 percent of all House seats.
7. Of course, Trump did lose the popular vote in 2016 nationally, and this is what the national election surveys seek to assess.
8. The basis for why the ANES sets the "gold standard" in survey research is developed in Appendix 1A to this chapter.
9. It may be that some state surveys were far off the mark, but we are studying the national electorate, not state electorates.
10. In addition to the NSF funding going to the university or universities that are home to the principal investigators (PIs), which in 2016 were the University of Michigan and Stanford University, the NSF requires the appointment of an advisory board to serve as intermediaries between the PIs on the one hand and the NSF and the general user community on the other. We mention that because the senior author served as chair of the board for the 2016 study. See electionstudies.org for more details.
11. See "American National Election Studies Competition, Program Solicitation, NSF 18-519," https://nsf.gov/pubs/2018/nsf18519/nsf18519.htm, accessed December 7, 2017. This document is the NSF's request for proposals for the 2020 ANES.
12. And to be sure, there are biases in surveys based on random sampling, especially with respect to convincing those sampled to agree to participate. These are generally smaller than the biases from opt-in features, and the ANES in particular, thanks to

144 NOTES

NSF funding, is about the best in getting those who are asked to participate to agree to be interviewed.

13. Two others we don't mention in much detail here are that the ANES generates proposals for questions from across the nation and even the world. That is, the survey reflects input from a wide array of scholars (and others) from a diverse set of backgrounds and disciplines. It thus has the strongest possible intellectual base. Second, the ANES invests considerable effort and resources in developing the highest quality survey instrument possible. Indeed, the survey that is focal to our analysis in the next chapter was a "pilot" survey designed for testing and refining new survey questions to ensure the highest possible quality. That test was a rigorous, high-quality national survey of its own, precisely to provide the best way to test the quality and usefulness of proposed new questions, but we exploit that aspect less and its being a full national survey more.

14. The online appendix can be accessed by searching for this book's title on the Oxford Academic platform, at academic.oup.com.

Chapter 2

1. Gallup began measuring the nation's opinions in 1935.
2. They argued that this was because the public had so little information about congressional candidates and campaigns that all voters had to bring to bear on the choice was their long-standing partisan affiliations. As we saw in the last chapter, shortly after Campbell and colleagues wrote this, the situation began to change as people became increasingly able to recognize the names of their incumbent House members, and a significant number of voters were willing to cross party lines to support the incumbent.
3. We define exactly what we mean by *fundamental* later in this chapter.
4. As we will see, although remaining moderate overall on most policies, voters are becoming more emotionally charged, which, when applied to partisanship, is called "affective partisanship" (Iyengar et al. 2019).
5. Quoted in Hamilton et al. ([1788] 1961, 78).
6. These cities were Sandusky, Ohio, featured in Lazarsfeld et al. (1948), and Elmira, New York, reported in Berelson et al. (1954).
7. Given the nature of the two small cities (Sandusky, Ohio, and Elmira, New York) studied, race, ethnicity, and the religious lines of cleavage we observe today were not politically relevant in the 1940s in small-city Ohio and New York.
8. *Religion* in their work meant the three mainstream religious categories (Protestant, Catholic, and Jew) rather than today's mainstream versus fundamentalist/born again divisions.
9. The word *fundamental* is borrowed from Aldrich et al. (2019), who in turn borrowed it from the macro-election-prediction tradition (see, e.g., Campbell 2008), but of course they borrowed the term from even earlier scholarship.

NOTES 145

10. They discuss ideology with a substantive, policy basis to it. We keep ideology and issues separate, in part because important scholarship provides different theoretical understandings of ideology and issues and in part because it permits the two to move with different dynamics. One of our main points is that the fundamentals once had diverse dynamics, but these are now converging toward a single dynamic.

11. That could be because they are directly causal of the vote, or (as in the case of party identification) because they affect other variables that in turn affect the vote (as per Stokes 1966, party identification shapes candidate evaluations, even if imperfectly, which in turn influence the vote). We think of estimating the direct effects of the fundamentals on the vote as something like a reduced-form estimation, able to include any direct and any indirect effects together.

12. The seven-point issue scales were first used in 1968 for two issues (the Vietnam War and urban unrest), and their popularity has led to their being one of the core measures of issues since then. Many of these issues were asked about in earlier elections using different questions, indicating that these particular issues were even more durable features of elections. That the ANES includes them as a core measure of electoral politics is relevant to the fourth criterion for being a fundamental force, as well.

13. Our measure of economic retrospective evaluations (Is the economy better or worse than a year ago?) is inherently tied to the current situation. What is durable and fundamental is the perpetual relevance of the economy. This measure is used because of its theoretical centrality in the relevant literature and frequent use in the ANES, but also because it does not ask about presidential, governmental, or party performance.

14. The particular measure available through multiple ANES surveys is called *racial resentment*. We discuss this at some length below. However, we warn the reader that this scale was developed primarily to measure White attitudes toward Black Americans. If there were a suitable measure designed for measuring "attitudes toward race" (whatever that might mean) for every respondent, we would be pleased to use it. But this measure is available and of durable importance for many respondents, including more than White respondents. It is also supplemented by racial categorization in the "demographics" that are included along with the fundamentals.

15. They used (and the rest of the world since then has used) the word *weak*, although that is not how the question is asked of respondents.

16. Their original account of partisanship was that it did *not* affect the vote directly but did so indirectly, through its effect on shaping voter evaluations of short-term forces, such as the candidates, parties as managers of government, and issues. Converse also proposed a dynamic equilibrium model of the development of partisanship in a democracy that presages the normal vote equilibrium (Converse 1969; updated in Aldrich et al. 2020, inter alia).

17. Partisanship was originally thought to develop in or around third grade; see, for example, Easton and Dennis ([1969] 1980) and Vaillancourt (1973).

18. Indeed, Von Neumann and Morgenstern (1944) needed to develop a theory of cardinal utility functions (i.e., those that include measures of strength of preference in an interval scale) for individuals before they could develop game theory.

146   NOTES

19. Ideology was measured indirectly in the earliest studies. Scholars based their "ide-ological innocence" arguments, for the most part, on responses to questions about what voters reported they "liked" or "disliked" about the candidates and parties in the election. In the 1960s the ANES began experimenting with seven-point issue scales, which became its standard issue scale in 1972, on which respondents could place themselves and their perceptions of where candidates stood on the issues. The virtue of this method of asking the question was to provide an immediate tie between the voters' sense of personal issue preferences and their understanding of political elites (see Aldrich and McKelvey 1977). Beginning in 1972, the ANES employed a compa-rable seven-point scale for measuring ideology, one that ran from extremely liberal (at point 1), through neither liberal nor conservative (at the midpoint, 4), to ex-tremely conservative (at point 7), along with questions concerning where candidates and parties stand on it. See the online appendix referred to in Chapter 1 for question wording.

20. By "near" they meant that there was some recognition of the notion but it was not suf-ficiently developed to be of much use.

21. We do have the advantage of two more elections to study, both of which yield the highest scores of relevance on ideology and its fundamental influence. In that sense, it is not a surprise that we find their "half empty" more like "half full." (In 2012, the party-ideology correlation then available for the researchers was .45 and the party-issues correlation was .39, much larger than in 1972 but considerably smaller than in 2020.)

22. See Figure 4.9 for details.

23. Which is not to say they did change for that reason, only that they knew what they were doing.

24. Clearly these are durable issues, extending in some cases back to debates between Hamiltonians and Jeffersonians.

25. For a brief review of the history of race in the United States and its applications to par-tisan politics, see Aldrich and Griffin (2017).

26. The scale itself was not included in the ANES until 1988, but it has been considered a core item since then, included in all subsequent surveys except in 1996. Despite the different labels, the content of the scale has not changed substantially over time.

27. "Apolitical" is measured by responses of "DK; NA; other; refused to answer; no" in the party identification battery.

28. As noted above, Goldwater voted against the Civil Rights Act of 1964, just as he was closing in on the Republican nomination that year. Presumably as a result, he won only his home state and states in the Deep South, embracing this possibility by being the first Republican presidential candidate to run a "southern strategy."

29. These data indicate that the long-term stability of party identification is not due to its being the "unmoved mover" it is sometimes claimed to be, but to its ability to respond, and quickly, to significant changes in politics that are directly relevant to voters.

30. See Berezow (2014).

31. There are many things that Democrats and Republicans in Congress and elsewhere agree upon. Many bills that pass do so with bipartisan support. What we see and hear

NOTES 147

about, however, are the matters that divide the parties. Candidates then focus their campaigns primarily on these partisan-dividing issues.

32. By "biases and heuristics" they meant cognitive shortcuts that could often be convenient and helpful but also could easily lead to incorrect choices.

33. The authors of *The American Voter* made this point clearly themselves (Campbell et al. 1960, 65). "Yet it is *not* true that attitudes toward the several elements of politics are only reflections of party loyalty or of group membership or of other factors that may lead to perceptual distortion. To suppose that they are is to understate the importance of changes in the properties of what the individual sees in his environment. Changes in the external realities of politics can have effects on popular feelings within every partisan or social grouping in the electorate. The truth of this statement is easily seen if we observe that attitudes toward the objects of politics, varying through time, can explain short-term fluctuations in partisan divisions of the vote, whereas partisan loyalties and social characteristics, which are relatively inert through time, account but poorly for these shifts" (emphasis in original).

34. Key (1966) argued that voters evaluated how well the incumbent had done in handling the economy and reasoned that "one good turn deserved another" or voted to "throw the rascal out," with the electorate serving as a "rational god of vengeance and of reward." Downs (1957) laid out an argument that Fiorina (1981) developed rigorously, in which voters looked at how the economy had done as a guide to what to expect in the future. The latter two also differed from Key in theorizing that voters made comparative assessments, examining how the incumbent party actually did compared to what they might expect the other party to have done were it in office.

35. And, as in Fiorina (1981), other circumstances than economic ones could be evaluated the same way, such as war or peace, in which "circumstances meant very complicated policies that could best be judged by their success or failure that was observable."

36. It could work even in Key's version, as Ferejohn (1986) demonstrated formally.

37. Our position is that presidents may not be able to guarantee a good economy, but they can certainly create a bad one.

38. The correlation between GDP growth rate and perceptions of the economy is 0.626 (p < 0.05) with a slope of 10.47.

Chapter 3

1. The Democratic Caucus (as the organization of House Democrats is called) found those actions and related ones beyond the pale even then. Several of the defectors were punished for those actions, such as the removal of Phil Gramm (D-TX) from a coveted seat on the Budget Committee.

2. Campbell et al. (1960) considered responses about economic conditions to be "unsophisticated" responses, in that they classified such responses as the fourth level of conceptualization, called the "nature of the times," which was only one step above "no issue content." These levels were derived from the open-ended responses to the "likes-dislikes" questions asked about the candidates and parties in the 1956 ANES.

148 NOTES

About a quarter of respondents (and of reported voters) fell into that category, but such nonideological responses that touched on the economy were but one way respondents discussed the nature of the times. As we saw in Chapter 2, scholars had studied the relationship between the economy and the vote for decades already, and it would become one of the largest areas of study in subsequent years. Perhaps had the economy not been quite so good that year, such responses would have seemed more substantial to these authors.

3. Note that having "only" a group basis for partisanship in the 1950s (and not ideology or public policy) is similar to what, two decades later, Conover and Feldman (1981) found about the ideology scale. One might argue, on the other hand, that a group basis for judgment, for example liking unions and knowing they support Democrats, might provide a clue as to where a union-endorsed Democratic candidate stands on policy. This is close to the essence of the Lupia and McCubbins (1998) account of how voters learn relevant political information. While it may well be true that group affect is a symbolic basis for ideology, as Conover and Feldman wrote, it may also be true that symbols can convey meaningful content, perhaps not in the 1970s, when they studied ideology, but perhaps in the twenty-first century when ideology and all such electoral matters appear to align with each other. Further, it is perhaps natural that there be a group basis to partisanship, inter alia, because the social-economic bases of politics that Lazarsfeld and colleagues (1968; Berelson et al. 1986) had studied were a major source of partisan orientations in the Campbell et al. (1960) account.

4. See Campbell et al. (1960, table 10-1, 249). As noted earlier, these scholars used survey responses to probes that asked for explanations of what respondents meant by what they liked and what they disliked about the two parties and the two presidential nominees.

5. The nine-in-ten calculation includes partisan leaners as partisans, leaving only the 8–12 percent of respondents categorized as "pure" independents outside of the partisan category.

6. Actually, the questions are asked and have been analyzed via an automated text analysis program for the 1984–2016 period. The authors found that the proportion of Democrats coded as actual or near ideologues has not changed much over time (still in the 10–15 percent range), but it has increased dramatically among Republicans. Their study found that between 20 and 30 percent of Republicans were coded as near or actual ideologues. See Allamong et al. (n.d.).

7. This is our averaging of the data reported issue by issue in Campbell et al. (1960, Table 8-3, 182).

8. And they included all seven-point issue scales with candidate placements asked in that election year, a number that ranged between seven and nine per election. All three issue scales included in PIP3 and the five in PIPER are also a part of these numbers.

9. This criterion was important to Campbell et al. (1960), as the above quotation suggests, but they did not have the data to examine it.

NOTES 149

10. The set of issues included does vary from year to year, including those that seemed particularly important that year but also policies with durable relevance, typically questions asked over many elections. The latter form our issue-scale fundamental.

11. See also Aldrich et al. (2019) for application of these criteria to the 11-point left-right scale used in the CSES (Comparative Study of Electoral Systems) module and thus used in a large number of nations.

12. They used responses to open-ended "likes" and "dislikes" questions about the parties and candidates and looked for evidence of ideology in those reported "likes" and "dislikes." Obviously, we might well expect most ideologues today to use ideological terms and thinking in determining what they like and dislike about the parties and their candidates. However, we can also imagine people responding with very different types of responses to what they like and dislike about Trump and/or his opponents. Apparent misuse of classified information on email servers or apparent commission of sexual assault do not strike us as "ideological," but do strike us as plausible bases of choice and certainly a plausible like or dislike.

13. The original criteria for issues voting were measured by whether the respondent gave a nonmissing (substantive opinion) response to the issue question, said they knew the party positions, and said they saw a difference between those positions. These are quite close to the same as the first three criteria used by Abramson and colleagues.

14. It was in fact the case that unprecedented proportions of respondents in 1976 placed Ford and Carter at the same point on many seven-point scales. They thus did not meet the "see a difference" criterion and could not vote on the basis of that issue. It could be, of course, that many saw no difference because the candidates did in fact take very similar stances on many issues that year.

15. If we use the strictest definition of enduring issues, the three seven-point scales that extend from their creation in 1972 to 2020, then 75 percent met the three criteria that Campbell et al. (1960) used, and 70 percent met all four criteria in 2020.

16. Their "total effects" results differ from those we report below. They directly relate party identification to the vote, which as we noted was (and still is) the disciplinary norm, and thus the results in Figure 3.3 are equivalent to the estimates of the short-term attitudes on the vote, parceled out among the three categories of measures. We followed Stokes et al. (1958) and Campbell et al. (1960) in modeling party identification as a long-term force that affected the six short-term attitudes but was not, in turn, affected by them. This position became referred to as party identification being the "unmoved mover."

17. We will discuss the full specifications shortly. For now, they include the various SES variables and the other fundamentals (but not short-term attitudes).

18. The detailed statistical results that underlie the figures can be found in our online appendix.

19. Technically, it is the difference between the predicted probability of the vote for a person with a fundamental score at the twenty-fifth percentile, holding all else equal at their means, compared to a voter at the seventy-fifth percentile, ceteris paribus.

20. Just why 2008 is relatively low is a mystery but may be due to the self-evidential nature of disastrous economic performance over the preceding year, and thus to the

150 NOTES

lower variance in the measure (i.e., almost everyone agreeing that the economy had worsened from 2007 to 2008).

21. We do not have observations of parental socialeconomic status or partisanship. Even respondent reports of parental SES and party ID are highly suspect and not regularly available. We do note that this means that the respondent's socioeconomic status and long-term attitudes must stand in for these prior variables.

22. Recall that racial resentment was not included in the 1996 ANES survey.

23. The rise in SES predicting the vote in 2008 and 2012 reflects at least in large part the enhanced relationship between race and the vote whether that meant being inclined to be for or against Obama.

24. Note that the government provision of health insurance question was not asked in 1980. Figures using PIP3 therefore do not have an entry for that year, even though we draw lines in figures from 1976 to 1984.

25. We ran a series of logit models, with our dependent variable coded 1 if the respondent reported voting for the Republican candidate and 0 if the respondent reported voting for the Democratic candidate. In addition to our fundamental forces, we include a number of standard demographic controls: age, race, gender, education, religiosity, and income level. We created a dummy variable for "highly religious" Protestants. Protestants are considered highly religious based on church attendance and the degree to which they believe religion guides their daily lives. Our fundamental forces, as well as religiosity and education, are coded on a 0–1 scale. Race, gender, and religiosity were treated as dummy variables. Ages range from eighteen to ninety-nine.

26. The health insurance question was not asked in 1980, and so in 1980 alone the scale actually consists of two questions (government provision of jobs and a standard of living plus aid to minorities).

Chapter 4

1. Or, more accurately, the set has expanded to five measured fundamentals. We suspect that both racial beliefs and retrospective evaluations of the economy were fundamental in the 1950s but were not measured until the 1980s. It is the ideological and issue fundamentals that appear to be the (only?) two to become relevant in or around the 1980s.

2. We emphasize that congressional "polarization" is actually *partisan* polarization. In any contended vote there is always some kind of polarization present. In the 1950s, for example, many votes showed an ideological polarization that was not also partisan. This form of polarization was referred to as the formation of a "conservative coalition" on the floor of Congress, aligning many (mostly southern) Democrats with Republicans and thus splitting the majority party. At issue here is a polarization that, first, divides Democrats from Republicans and second, is a consistent division across policies and over time. Unless indicated otherwise, we use the terms *partisan polarization* and more simply *polarization* as synonyms in this book.

NOTES 151

3. We will also see, however, at least some indications that the electorate may be beginning to become more extreme on some of these issues (especially partisanship and racial resentment).

4. Actually, some nearly unanimous votes have also been dropped for technical reasons, see voteview.com.

5. That interpretation is an (often well-justified) inference, which Poole and Rosenthal (1987) support with additional evidence. Still, the technique is not one that directly estimates liberal-conservative scores. Two legislators end up with DW-NOMINATE scores that put them very far away from each other because they rarely vote the same, whereas those who do vote the same almost all the time end up with nearly identical scores. What those scores mean, however, is interpretation added to what the scaling procedure calculates. Thus, for example, Lee (2009) argues that it is a partisan dimension as much as, or maybe even more than, it is an ideological dimension, and Figure 4.1 thus illustrates times in which Democrats tend to vote together more often, giving them similar scores, and vote in opposition to Republicans, giving the Democrats different scores from the Republicans, as discussed in the next paragraph in the text. In other words, the same scaling results, as reported in the figure can be understood as indicating ideological voting or indicating partisan voting.

6. Note that the y axis in the figure runs from 0.5 to 0.9, less than the full range of potential values of party difference (which can in principle range from 0.0 to about 2.0). The reported range maximizes the clarity of the variation, even though the range of actual observations is about a quarter of the total logically possible.

7. More accurately, we use 218 from 1912 on, that is, since the House had 435 members, and we use whatever forms a simple majority when the House had a different number of seats.

8. The surveys generally included a follow-up question of whether they saw one party as more conservative than the other, and if so, which party is the more conservative. In all available years, about seven in eight who reported seeing a difference correctly identified the Republican Party as the more conservative. In 2020 this reached a peak of 79 percent of respondents. Of course, this peak in accuracy comes on top of an increasing percentage who say they see a difference. At this point, it is approaching nearly every respondent saying they see a difference and correctly identifying the GOP as the more conservative choice.

9. Thus, for example, a Strong Democrat is scored as "0" on the party identification scale, while a Strong Republican is scored as "1," with "pure" Independents coded as "0.5," and so on. Both our issue and racial resentment scales are created from a set of variables that is then scaled to the similar 0 to 1 range. Specific details may be found in the online appendix.

10. The year 1980 featured double-digit inflation, unemployment, and interest rates; 1992 was a short but sharp recession that, it should be noted, had mostly ended by election day, although not to George H. W. Bush's benefit; 2008 was, of course, the start of the Great Recession.

11. We exclude economic retrospection because the public's overall responses vary, due in large part to the changing economic conditions.

152 NOTES

12. All surveys of the electorate gather data on partisanship. Racial resentment is not asked as regularly, so we must await more substantial data collection to assess what its future trajectory might look like.
13. Like partisanship, there is a distinct change from 2016 to 2020. The distribution overall is of a less resentful public in 2020 than in 2016 but with the emergence of modes at the two extremes.
14. Economic retrospection is dominated by movement in line with changing circumstances in the national economy.
15. Any growth in more extreme responses to racial resentment therefore appears to be due to Democrats. Of course Blacks voters were overwhelmingly Democrats before this time series began, so the change is presumably due to some combination of increasing numbers of other racial and ethnic minorities becoming Democrats (and presumably being less racially resentful) and White Democrats consisting of increasing numbers of the less resentful (such as is often found among more educated citizens, a growing proportion of whom are Democrats).
16. These five are party identification and ideology from PIP3, an enhanced five-issue policy scale, economic retrospection, and the racial resentment scale.
17. These are the three appropriate for this procedure. Obviously, partisanship is used in each one, and the nature of the economic retrospection question obviates its use in this way.
18. The Poole-Rosenthal scaling analyzing members of Congress's roll call voting patterns yields positions that are mostly concentrated in scores that run from -1.5 to $+1.5$, more than twice as far as our rescaling of the seven-point ANES ideology scale to a 0–1 range. Figure 4.13 reports the difference in party means for each Congress.
19. The average rate of increase for the two lines in Figure 3.10 is nearly identical: 2.08% for our DW-NOMINATE score and 5.14% for the seven-point ideology measure.
20. We examine partisanship in this regard for two reasons. Partisanship figures more prominently in electoral behavior research generally and will play a greater role than any of the other fundamentals in our account, as we will show later. We also have considerable amounts of relevant data to evaluate compared to racial resentment, the other somewhat polarizing fundamental.

Chapter 5

1. We addressed more cognitive components of the fundamentals throughout earlier chapters. Issues are missing from this set. They tend to be studied in more cognitive than affective terms, although anyone who thinks seriously about the role of, say, pro-life and pro-choice politics of abortion in America would believe, as we do, that issues have strong affective components as well.
2. See Huddy (2001) for an especially important, indeed a seminal, contribution.
3. We'd like to report that her findings illustrate the growing influence of the increasing number and overlapping-ness of the other fundamentals on partisanship, but we lack the data to illustrate that. So we leave it as a conjecture.

NOTES 153

4. Although there are affective components, certainly to party identification measures, among the fundamentals. Affect and cognition cannot be simply or easily disentangled.

5. According to Stokes, none of the other short-term attitudes—toward the parties, toward other political groups, toward domestic issues, or toward foreign affairs—showed similar variability over time.

6. Because respondents are drawn from a random sample of eligible voters throughout the nation, quality sampling can support inferences to and about the nation.

7. This is true even with what is called a "cluster sample," used by the ANES. In cluster designs, randomization occurs in several ways. First a relatively small number of clusters of geographic locations are drawn at random, and then respondents are drawn, also at random, from within those various clusters. The key for a high-quality survey to be able to support inferences about the population is that the probability of any citizen being sampled is known (or at least knowable), but unlike a *simple* random sample, the probabilities need not be the same across all of those eligible for being sampled.

8. We specify our model as do Jacobson and Carson, although we differ by including the fundamentals we have used in this study (which are different from theirs), and our demographic variables are at least somewhat different, too, to remain consistent with our studies of the presidential vote and candidate evaluations. In other words, we did not try to replicate their analyses exactly.

9. Note that incumbency has an advantage in that it is a "hard" measure, rather than a respondent report from the same survey, and thus can be considered "exogenous" to the rest of the survey responses, including the questions that make up the fundamentals. (Of course it is associated with party identification, so that we can know if the incumbent is of the same party as the respondent or not, and that a respondent's survey response is part of the fundamentals.)

10. Recall also that the full set is not included in the 1996 survey either.

11. To be sure, this is "predicting" the congressional vote in presidential election years. The NSF declined to support midterm congressional surveys after the turn of this century, in otherwise generously and consistently funding the ANES. Thus the ANES has not been able to conduct congressional election midterm surveys since 2002 (it used money from a different source in that year), so we cannot be sure what has happened in the midterm election years. We suspect that they follow a similar pattern, but we are exploring ways to make this more precise and observable.

12. Note that we "drew" the lines in the figure between the 1992 to the 2000 elections, even though 1996 is not available.

13. This does not prove that fundamentals are the driving force, the "cause" of the congressional vote. It does suggest that this is a hypothesis worth trying to establish more firmly, and that doing so might well yield a positive result.

14. Recall, however, that they remain significant factors in the congressional vote even if they do not increase the explanatory power much above what the fundamentals alone provide.

154 NOTES

15. These vary from 0 to 1. The higher the score the more the variation in the thermometer score is "explained" by the fundamentals. Note also that in both years, Democrats outstripped Republicans on these measures, quite possibly because of the fact of a simpler, two-candidate contest being easier to figure out.

16. Interestingly, Carter and Reagan in 1980 were the two least popular nominees recorded until 2016, in spite of their being rather popularly received by both parties in the early nomination campaign.

17. It is also important to note that the more ideological the candidate (Kennedy and Sanders on the Democratic side, Reagan and Cruz on the Republican side), the more fully did the electorate use ideology in evaluating these candidates. That is, it appears that the public is, sensibly enough, using ideology when the candidate is a more extreme ideologue and thus ideology is a more useful criterion.

18. Famously, Reagan did invite voters to hold Carter responsible in the general election, asking voters at the presidential debate whether they were better off today than they were four years earlier.

19. John E. "Jeb" Bush is an exception, perhaps because his already foundering campaign failed to excite Republicans at all and attracted some Democratic-leaning support as, at the time, the closest to a "bipartisan" Republican measured in the survey.

20. This can be seen in the increases in the R-squared term of about .07 and .05 for Trump and Sanders, respectively.

21. It is also a substantial predictor for Cruz and even for Rubio, as well as for Carson and Fiorina, but not others.

22. Recall that the scale is designed to measure White people's attitudes toward Black people.

23. The race of the respondent does not affect evaluations of any Republican (except for a modest effect for Hispanics in evaluating Bush more positively), whether one includes the racial resentment scale or not. Note that that comment about Bush also means that Hispanics do not rate Trump more negatively than others, ceteris paribus, statements about a wall on the southern border (and why) to the contrary notwithstanding. (Note also that the anti-immigration questions we study in the fall survey were not included in this January survey.) On the Democratic side, Black respondents were significantly more likely to evaluate Clinton positively, and White respondents to evaluate Sanders modestly more positively, with or without controlling for racial resentment.

24. Anti-immigrant sentiments are also a part of populism, but that concept has a number of other dimensions as well (see, e.g., Mudd and Kaltwassar 2017).

25. We measure populism with a scale variable created from a battery of questions tapping into respondents' attitudes about majority rule, political corruption, and political compromise.

26. The question reads: "So far as you and your family are concerned, how worried are you about your current financial situation? [Extremely worried, very worried, moderately worried, a little worried, or not at all worried/Not at all worried, a little worried, moderately worried, very worried, or extremely worried?]."

NOTES   155

27. "'Most politicians are trustworthy.' (Do you [agree strongly, agree somewhat, neither agree nor disagree, disagree somewhat, or disagree strongly/disagree strongly, disagree somewhat, neither agree nor disagree, agree somewhat or agree strongly.)" Note that while anti-immigrant sentiment and populism are measured by a battery of questions, both distrust of politicians and economic anxiety are measured by single questions. Although a battery might be preferred, both questions are high in face validity: they directly target each concept.

28. Authoritarianism: (1) "Please tell me which one you think is more important for a child to have: Independence or respect for elders," (2) "(Which one is more important for a child to have): Curiosity or good manners," (3) "(Which one is more important for a child to have): Obedience or self-reliance," 4) "(Which one is more important for a child to have): Being considerate or well behaved." Aldrich, Hillygus and Zhou (2018) report a Cronbach's alpha of .65 for this scale, which indicates reasonable internal reliability.

29. (1) "And now thinking specifically about immigrants. (Do you [agree strongly, agree somewhat, neither agree nor disagree, disagree somewhat, or disagree strongly/disagree strongly, disagree somewhat, neither agree nor disagree, agree somewhat or agree strongly] with the following statement?) 'Immigrants are generally good for America's economy.'" (2) "(Do you [agree strongly, agree somewhat, neither agree nor disagree, disagree somewhat, or disagree strongly/disagree strongly, disagree somewhat, neither agree nor disagree, agree somewhat or agree strongly] with the following statement?) 'America's culture is generally harmed by immigrants.'" (3) "(Do you [agree strongly, agree somewhat, neither agree nor disagree, disagree somewhat, or disagree strongly/disagree strongly, disagree somewhat, neither agree nor disagree, agree somewhat or agree strongly] with the following statement?) 'Immigrants increase crime rates in the United States.'" (4) "Some people say that the following things are important for being truly American. Others says they are not important. How important do you think the following is for being truly American . . . [very important, fairly important, not very important, or not important at all/ not important at all, not very important, fairly important or very important]? To have been born in the United States." (5) "(How important do you think the following is for being truly American . . . [very important, fairly important, not very important, or not important at all / not important at all, not very important, fairly important or very important]?) To have American ancestry." (6) "(How important do you think the following is for being truly American . . . [very important, fairly important, not very important, or not important at all/not important at all, not very important, fairly important or very important]?) To be able to speak English." (7) "(How important do you think the following is for being truly American . . . [very important, fairly important, not very important, or not important at all / not important at all, not very important, fairly important or very important]?) To follow America's customs and traditions." According to Aldrich et al. (2019), the Cronbach's alpha is .84, or an "excellent" level of internal relatability.

30. This scale consists of three questions from the larger scale addressing the following concerns: "Media should pay less attention to discrimination against women";

156   NOTES

"Women complaining about discrimination causes more problems"; "Women are seeking special favors."

31. The question about the video first asked if they had heard about the video, then the respondents who had heard of the video were asked: "Does [the video] matter: 1) a great deal; 2) a lot; 3) a moderate amount; 4) a little; or 5) not at all."

32. We use three that are regularly repeated: "really cares about people like me," "provides strong leadership," "knowledgeable." Others are used from time to time as they seem particularly relevant to the matchup of candidates that year. These three are, in a sense then, "fundamental" factors of evaluation, at least as inferred from their consistent usage, but they are very different from one election to the next, because each candidate varies a great deal from others on these traits.

33. In this sense, it is expectations about the office that are persistently consequential and fundamental.

34. We want to be clear. We began this investigation assuming that the traits would provide insight into how candidate evaluations modify the influence of the fundamentals on vote choice. We developed our thinking about these as a mixture of individual and institutional assessments as the project developed. Thus, the data analyses presented here should be understood as how we came to develop these theoretical ideas, not as how we are testing hypotheses derived from such a theory.

35. Note that 1996 is excluded due to the absence of the racial resentment scale that year. Note also that we use a very small range of 80–100 percent for the vertical axis in Figure 5.10 so the reader can visualize the small differences.

36. The full series of correlations is: 1980, .52; 1984, .62; 1988, .58; 1992, .60; 1996, .64; 2000, .64; 2004, .71; 2008, .66; 2012, .73; 2016, .73; 2020, .80.

37. A fuller explanation of the mediation results may be found in the appendix to this chapter.

38. For example, in 1988 the average direct effect of the fundamentals variable on the vote choice is 0.171, while it decreases to 0.142 in 2020. On the other hand, the total effect of both the fundamentals and trait scale on the vote choice increases from 0.307 in 1988 to 0.376 in 2020. Hence the increase in proportion that is mediated by the trait scale over time, since the estimate of the fundamentals' variable is decreasing, and the total variance explained by both traits is increasing. The indirect effect of the trait scale variable is 0.136 in 1988 and 0.234 in 2020.

Chapter 6

1. That brief moment was when southern Democrats defected from their party to support Republican proposals and defeat their own party's. In that sense, the Republicans held a working majority for a very brief period but did not hold a partisan majority until 1995.

2. Bill Clinton was the president, meaning the Republicans' congressional majorities had to work with his administration. They were able to get him to compromise heavily

NOTES   157

in their direction on several important measures such as, to paraphrase Clinton, "ending welfare as we know it."

3. See Aldrich and Griffin (2017) and sources cited therein. Note that the Jim Crow Museum at Ferris State University lists the Jim Crow period as running from 1877 to 1964 (https://www.ferris.edu/HTMLS/news/jimcrow/timeline/jimcrow.htm, accessed 4 3 2023).

4. After *Smith v. Allwright* (1944) ruled Whites-only primaries unconstitutional, southern Democratic primaries were no longer legally Whites only but were effectively so for decades thereafter, just as was the general electorate.

5. The North in the 1850s consisted primarily of the Northeast and what was to become the industrial Midwest, especially states around the Great Lakes.

6. Nelson Rockefeller was a major figure in this group and thus became their namesake. He was a grandson of John D. Rockefeller and a millionaire many times over himself, of course, but also had been governor of New York (1959–73) and vice president (1974–77). Members of group were also sometimes referred to as "Wall Street" as opposed to "main street" Republicans. Wall Street Republicans signified not just support for big business but also internationalism in their economic outlook, at least as compared to the more small-town and small-business-oriented "main street" Republicans, who tended to oppose international trade, economic collaborations, and related international and financial institutions

7. An individual might change to have their preferences come into alignment consistent with sorting. In fact, it may well be that "replacement" rather than "conversion" is the more common way that sorting happened. For example, a White southern Democrat might have been conservative on most fundamentals in the 1950s and 1960s even though a Democrat, perhaps even a "Reagan Democrat," who voted for Republicans for president without changing their Democratic Party identification. Perhaps she never changed even when it was possible to do so But her daughter might well have grown up with the same positions on the fundamentals but in a two-party South and therefore identified as a Republican from the outset, thus aligning all fundamentals.

8. That is the actual term they use (see Poole and Rosenthal 1987; Rosenthal 1992).

9. To be sure, there are very few variables for PIP3 and not that many more for PIPER. Those who use this technique frequently suggest that one needs more variables than we have at hand to be confident that they compose only one dimension. But we can only look at what we have, and we therefore can conclude that we have at least one dimension and, more weakly, we have no evidence in support of a second dimension. We note, further, that the evidence is so consistent over time and over all available measures that we have reasonable confidence that our inferences are justified.

10. This is akin to the R-squared values reported elsewhere in this book.

11. The absolute minimum for a three-variable model is that the first dimension must, by construction, account for one-third of the variance (for the five-variable model, it is a 20 percent minimum), and thus a one-dimensional model must account for substantially more than that minimum to count as truly one dimensional.

12. This is more commonly done with respect to the statistical technique known as factor analysis. The two are very similar mathematically, but they do differ.

158 NOTES

13. We can go a little further. If there were a competing second dimension, it would be one in which at least two of the variables contribute importantly. If it were composed only of a single variable, it would not be so much a second dimension as a measure of the idiosyncratic effect of that unique, single variable. We find the latter. Both PIP3 and PIPER illustrate nearly textbook-level patterns in which any possible dimension beyond the first is typically dominated solely by a large coefficient for a single variable.

14. The organization did not call it "polarization"; indeed, the idea was so foreign in American politics at that time as not to be considered in these terms.

15. This is so because the public is not divided into exactly two opposing camps on policies, but typically has a large middle and two smaller (if substantial) blocks toward the two extremes. Thus, any policy chosen will not be one preferred by a majority of the public. Of course, we might say, most of the time in recent years no party has had unified control of the government for long (and the 2010 and 2018 elections are a good measure of how the public acts when faced with the prospect of retaining one party with unified control). Perhaps divided government is the American solution (see Mayhew 1991).

16. If we take that to be what the data show.

17. Perhaps better said, his contributions in nos. 10 and 51 are singularly important together.

18. He coupled majority rule in elections with, in between elections, impeachment proceedings reflecting separated but intermingled powers pitting one set of ambitious politicians against another, until such time as a new electoral majority could remove the tyrannical incumbents. Note that one did not have to have a well-defined majority for elections to work. If a minority government was tyrannizing over a majority, that majority could agree to "vote the rascals out" of office without agreeing on a positive majority; that is what they would like to do when in office. See Riker (1982) for development of this argument.

19. A small number of mountain districts (typically 3 or 4 of the over 120 House districts in the South) supported the Republicans, but that was true nowhere else in the South.

20. What European's call liberal is what Americans call conservative, or perhaps libertarian.

21. Belgium set a record of 652 days of trying to form a government after the elections in 2019.

22. Italy's circumstances for decades.

23. Of course, the socioeconomic and demographic variables tap many of the politically relevant trait cleavages.

24. Thus, as crystallization indicates, the definition and measurement of cleavages are from the very beginning completely distinct from a correlation analysis. By assessing the cleavage structure of the fundamentals, therefore, we are adding something new to the correlational and PCA analysis earlier in the chapter.

25. Only points 1 and 7 are labeled on the respondents' cards, however.

26. Some issues lend themselves to identity type groupings, such as, say, pro-life and pro-choice. Others are not as directly related to issue-based groups defining that issue-based cleavage.

27. This steep decline is also when the various indicators of "affective partisanship" began their steepest decline. This is not a coincidence. Rather, it is a key indicator of the close relationship between political substance and emotion.

Chapter 7

1. Indeed, as we pointed out earlier, it is a fool's errand to imagine that we can distinguish that sharply between affect and cognition, substance and emotion. They are inextricably bound, some even claiming that to be true in time measured in fractions of a second.

References

Abelson, Robert P., Donald R. Kinder, Mark D. Peters, and Susan T. Fiske. 1982. "Affective and Semantic Components in Political Person Perception." *Journal of Personality and Social Psychology* 42 (4): 619.

Abramowitz, Alan I. 2013. *The Polarized Public? Why American Government Is So Dysfunctional.* Upper Saddle River, NJ: Pearson.

Abramowitz, Alan I., and Kyle L. Saunders. 2008. "Is Polarization a Myth?" *Journal of Politics* 70 (2): 542–555.

Achen, Christopher H., and Larry M. Bartels. 2016. *Democracy for Realists: Why Elections Do Not Produce Responsive Government.* Princeton, NJ: Princeton University Pres.

Aldrich, John H. 2011. *Why Parties? A Second Look.* Chicago: University of Chicago Press.

Aldrich, John H., Bradford H. Bishop, Rebecca S. Hatch, D. Sunshine Hillygus, and David W. Rohde. 2014. "Blame, Responsibility, and the Tea Party in the 2010 Midterm Elections." *Political Behavior* 36:471–491.

Aldrich, John H., Austin Bussing, Arvind Krishnamurthy, Nicolas Madan, Katelyn Mehling Ice, Kristen M. Renberg, and Hannah M. Ridge. 2020. "Does a Partisan Public Increase Democratic Stability?" In *Research Handbook on Political Partisanship,* edited by Henrik Oscarsson and Soren Holmberg, 256–265. Cheltenham, UK: Edward Elgar.

Aldrich, John H., Jamie L. Carson, Brad T. Gomez, and David W. Rohde. 2019. *Change and Continuity in the 2016 and 2018 Elections.* Thousand Oaks: CQ Press.

Aldrich, John H., and John D. Griffin. *Why Parties Matter: Political Competition and Democracy in the American South.* Chicago: University of Chicago Press, 2019.

Aldrich, John H., D. Sunshine Hillygus, and Jack Zhou. 2019. "Understanding the Trump Win: Populism, Partisanship, and Polarization in the 2016 Election." In *The Comeback of Populism: Transatlantic Perspectives,* edited by Heike Paul, Ursula Prutsch, and Jurgen Gebhardt, 65–87. Heidelberg, Germany: Universitatsverlag, Winter.

Aldrich, John H., and Richard D. McKelvey. 1977. "A Method of Scaling with Applications to the 1968 and 1972 Presidential Elections." *American Political Science Review* 71 (1): 111–130.

Allamong, Maxwell B., Benjamin Beutel, Jongwoo Jeong, and Paul M. Kellstedt. n.d. "The Evolution of Partisanship in America? Open-Ended Survey Responses and Partisan Conceptualizations in a Polarized Era." Working paper.

American Political Science Association. 1951. "Toward a More Responsible Two-Party System." *American Political Science Review* 44 (Sep., 1950): 536–541.

Arrow, Kenneth J. 1963. *Social Choice and Individual Values: New York.* New Haven: Yale University Press.

Baron, Reuben M., and David A. Kenny. 1986. "The Moderator–Mediator Variable Distinction in Social Psychological Research: Conceptual, Strategic, and Statistical Considerations." *Journal of Personality and Social Psychology* 51 (6): 1173.

162 REFERENCES

Berelson, Bernard R., Paul F. Lazarsfeld, and William N. McPhee. (1954) 1986. *Voting: A Study of Opinion Formation in a Presidential Campaign.* Chicago: University of Chicago Press.

Berezow, Alex. 2014. "Are Liberals or Conservatives More Anti-Vaccine?" Real Clear Science, October 20. https://www.realclearscience.com/journal_club/2014/10/20/are_liberals_or_conservatives_more_anti-vaccine_108905.html.

Bolsen, Toby, and Risa Palm. 2019. "Motivated Reasoning and Political Decision Making." In *Oxford Research Encyclopedia of Politics.* Oxford, England: Oxford University Press.

Brady, David W. 1973. *Congressional Voting in a Partisan Era: A Study of the McKinley Houses and a Comparison to the Modern House of Representatives.* Lawrence: University Press of Kansas.

Brady, David W. 1988. *Critical Elections and Congressional Policy Making.* Vol. 1. Stanford, CA: Stanford University Press.

Campbell, Angus, Philip E. Converse, Warren E. Miller, and Donald E. Stokes. 1960. *The American Voter.* New York: Wiley.

Campbell, Angus, Philip E. Converse, Warren E. Miller, and Donald E. Stokes. 1966. *Elections and the Political Order.* New York: Wiley.

Campbell, Angus, Gerald Gurin, and Warren Miller. 1954. *The Voter Decides.* Evanston, IL: Row, Peterson.

Campbell, James E. 2008. "The Trial-Heat Forecast of the 2008 Presidential Vote: Performance and Value Considerations in an Open-Seat Election." *PS: Political Science & Politics* 41 (4): 697–701.

Campbell, James E. 2016. *Polarized: Making Sense of a Divided America.* Princeton, NJ: Princeton University Press.

Cohen, Claire. November 7, 2020. "Donald Trump Sexism Tracker: Every Offensive Comment in One Place." https://www.telegraph.co.uk/women/politics/donald-trump-sexism-tracker-every-offensive-comment-in-one-place/

Conover, Pamela Johnston, and Stanley Feldman. 1981. "The Origins and Meaning of Liberal/Conservative Self-Identifications." *American Journal of Political Science* 25 (4): 617–645.

Converse, Philip E. 1966. "The Concept of a Normal Vote." In *Elections and the Political Order,* edited by Angus Campbell, Philip E. Converse, Warren E. Miller, and Donald E. Stokes, 93–99. New York: Cambridge University Press.

Converse, Philip E. 1969. "Of Time and Partisan Stability." *Comparative Political Studies* 2 (2): 139–171.

Converse, Philip E. 1970. "Attitudes and Non-attitudes: Continuation of a Dialogue." *Quantitative Analysis of Social Problems* 168:189.

Converse, Philip E. 2006. "The Nature of Belief Systems in Mass Publics (1964)." *Critical Review* 18 (1–3): 1–74.

Dawson, Michael C. 1995. *Behind the Mule: Race and Class in African-American Politics.* Princeton, NJ: Princeton University Press.

Duch, Raymond M., and Randy Stevenson. 2006. "Assessing the Magnitude of the Economic Vote over Time and across Nations." *Electoral Studies* 25 (3): 528–547.

Duch, Raymond M., and Randolph T. Stevenson. 2008. *The Economic Vote: How Political and Economic Institutions Condition Election Results.* Cambridge: Cambridge University Press.

Duch, Raymond M., and Randy Stevenson. 2010. "The Global Economy, Competency, and the Economic Vote." *Journal of Politics* 72 (1): 105–123.

REFERENCES   163

Easton, David, and Jack Dennis. (1969) 1980. *Children in the Political System: Origins of Political Legitimacy*. Chicago: University of Chicago Press.

Erikson, Robert S., Michael B. MacKuen, and James A. Stimson. 1998. "What Moves Macropartisanship? A Response to Green, Palmquist, and Schickler." *American Political Science Review* 92 (4): 901–912.

Erikson, Robert S., Michael B. MacKuen, and James A. Stimson. 2002. *The Macro Polity*. Cambridge: Cambridge University Press.

Festinger, Leon. 1962. "Cognitive Dissonance." *Scientific American* 207 (4): 93–106.

Fiorina, Morris P. 1981. *Retrospective Voting in American National Elections*. New Haven, CT: Yale University Press.

Fiorina, Morris P. 2017. *Unstable Majorities: Polarization, Party Sorting, and Political Stalemate*. Stanford CA: Hoover Institution Press.

Fiorina, Morris P., Samuel J. Abrams, and Jeremy Pope. 2006. *Culture War? The Myth of a Polarized America*. Longman Publishing.

Fowler, Anthony, and Andrew B. Hall. 2018. "Do Shark Attacks Influence Presidential Elections? Reassessing a Prominent Finding on Voter Competence." *Journal of Politics* 80 (4): 1423–1437.

Green, Donald P., Bradley Palmquist, and Eric Schickler. 2002. *Partisan Hearts and Minds: Political Parties and the Social Identities of Voters*. New Haven, CT: Yale University Press.

Greenwald, Anthony G., and David L. Ronis. 1978. "Twenty Years of Cognitive Dissonance: Case Study of the Evolution of a Theory." *Psychological Review* 85 (1): 53.

Hamilton, Alexander, James Madison, and John Jay. *The Federalist Papers*. New York: Mentor, 1961.

Hartwig, Frederick, William R. Jenkins, and Earl M. Temchin. 1980. "Variability in Electoral Behavior: The 1960, 1968, and 1976 Elections." *American Journal of Political Science* 24 (3): 553–558.

Henry, Patrick J., and David O. Sears. 2002. "The Symbolic Racism 2000 Scale." *Political Psychology* 23 (2): 253–283.

Hibbs, Douglas A., and Douglas A. Hibbs Jr. 1989. *The American Political Economy: Macroeconomics and Electoral Politics*. Cambridge: Harvard University Press.

Hetherington, Marc J. 2009 "Review Article: Putting Polarization in Perspective." *British Journal of Political Science* 39 (2): 413–448.

Huddy, Leonie. 2001. "From Social to Political Identity: A Critical Examination of Social Identity Theory." *Political Psychology* 22 (1): 127–156.

Imai, Kosuke, Luke Keele, and Dustin Tingley. 2010. "A General Approach to Causal Mediation Analysis." *Psychological Methods* 15 (4): 309–334.

Iyengar, Shanto, Yphtach Lelkes, Matthew Levendusky, Neil Malhotra, and Sean J. Westwood. 2019. "The Origins and Consequences of Affective Polarization in the United States." *Annual Review of Political Science* 22:129–146.

Jacobson, Gary C. 2015. "It's Nothing Personal: The Decline of the Incumbency Advantage in US House Elections." *Journal of Politics* 77 (3): 861–873.

Jacobson, Gary C., and Jamie L. Carson. 2015. *The Politics of Congressional Elections*. 9th ed. Lanham: Rowman & Littlefield.

Jacobson, Gary C., and Jamie L. Carson. 2019. *The Politics of Congressional Elections*. 10th ed. Lanham: Rowman & Littlefield.

Jardina, Ashley. 2019. *White Identity Politics*. Cambridge University Press.

164 REFERENCES

Jardina, Ashley, and Spencer Piston. 2023. "The Politics of Racist Dehumanization in the United States." *Annual Review of Political Science* 26:369--388.

Jennings, M. Kent, and Richard G. Niemi. 1968. "The Transmission of Political Values from Parent to Child." *American Political Science Review* 62 (1): 169–184.

Johannes, John R., and John C. McAdams. 1981. "The Congressional Incumbency Effect: Is It Casework, Policy Compatibility, or Something Else? An Examination of the 1978 Election." *American Journal of Political Science* 25 (3): 512–542.

Jones, Jeffery. January 17, 2022. "U.S. Political Party Preferences Shifted Greatly During 2021." https://news.gallup.com/poll/388781/political-party-preferences-shifted-grea tly-during-2021.aspx

Kahneman, Daniel, Paul Slovic, and Amos Tversky, eds. *Judgment under Uncertainty: Heuristics and Biases*. New York: Cambridge University Press.

Keith, Bruce E., David B. Magleby, Candice J. Nelson, Elizabeth A. Orr, and Mark C. Westlye. 1992. *The Myth of the Independent Voter*. Berkeley, CA: University of California Press.

Kinder, Donald R. 1983a. "Diversity and Complexity in American Public Opinion." In *Political Science: The State of the Discipline*, edited by Ada W. Finifter, 389–425. Washington, DC: APSA.

Kinder, Donald R. 1983b. *Presidential Traits*. ANES Pilot Study Report, No. nes002244. https://electionstudies.org/papers-documents/pilot-study-reports/.

Kinder, Donald R., and Nathan P. Kalmoe. 2017. *Neither Liberal nor Conservative: Ideological Innocence in the American Public*. Chicago, IL: University of Chicago Press.

Kramer, Gerald H. 1971. "Short-Term Fluctuations in US Voting Behavior, 1896–1964." *American Political Science Review* 65 (1): 131–143.

Kramer, Gerald H. 1983. "The Ecological Fallacy Revisited: Aggregate- versus Individual-Level Findings on Economics and Elections, and Sociotropic Voting." *American Political Science Review* 77 (1): 92–111.

Kteily, Nour S., and Emile Bruneau. 2017. "Darker Demons of Our Nature: The Need to (Re) Focus Attention on Blatant Forms of Dehumanization." *Current Directions in Psychological Science* 26 (6): 487–494.

Lane, Robert Edwards. 1962. *Political Ideology: Why the American Common Man Believes What He Does*. Glencoe, IL: The Free Press of Glencoe.

Lazarsfeld, Paul F., Bernard Berelson, and Hazel Gaudet. (1948) 1968. *The People's Choice: How the Voter Makes Up His Mind in a Presidential Campaign*. New York: Columbia University Press.

Lee, Frances E. 2009. *Beyond ideology: Politics, Principles, and Partisanship in the US Senate*. Chicago, IL: University of Chicago Press.

Levendusky, Matthew. 2009. *The Partisan Sort: How Liberals Became Democrats and Conservatives Became Republicans*. Chicago, IL: University of Chicago Press.

Lewis, Jeffrey B., Keith Poole, Howard Rosenthal, Adam Boche, Aaron Rudkin, and Luke Sonnet. 2023. *Voteview: Congressional Roll-Call Votes Database*. https://voteview.com/.

Lewis-Beck, Michael S. 1990. *Economics and Elections: The Major Western Democracies*. Ann Arbor, MI: University of Michigan Press.

Lewis-Beck, Michael S., and Mary Stegmaier. 2000. "Economic Determinants of Electoral Outcomes." *Annual Review of Political Science* 3 (1): 183–219.

Lijphart, Arend. (1968) 1975. *The Politics of Accommodation: Pluralism and Democracy in the Netherlands*. Vol. 142. Berkeley, CA: University of California Press.

REFERENCES 165

Lipset, Seymour Martin, and Stein Rokkan, eds. 1967a. *Party Systems and Voter Alignments: Cross-National Perspectives*. Vol. 7. New York: Free Press.

Lipset, Seymour Martin, and Stein Rokkan. 1967b. *Cleavage Structures, Party Systems, and Voter Alignments: An Introduction*. New York: Free Press.

Lodge, Milton, and Charles S. Taber. 2013. *The Rationalizing Voter*. Cambridge, UK: Cambridge University Press.

Lupia, Arthur, and Mathew D. McCubbins. 1998. *The Democratic Dilemma: Can Citizens Learn What They Need to Know?* Cambridge, UK: Cambridge University Press.

Mann, Thomas E., and Norman J. Ornstein. 2012. *It's Even Worse Than It Looks: How the American Constitutional System Collided with the New Politics of Extremism*. New York: Basic Books.

Margolis, Michael. 1977. "From Confusion to Confusion: Issues and the American Voter (1956–1972)." *American Political Science Review* 71 (1): 31–43.

Mason, Lilliana. 2018. *Uncivil Agreement: How Politics Became Our Identity*. Chicago, IL: University of Chicago Press.

McClain, Paula D., Jessica D. Johnson Carew, Eugene Walton Jr., and Candis S. Watts. 2009. "Group Membership, Group Identity, and Group Consciousness: Measures of Racial Identity in American Politics?" *Annual Review of Political Science* 12:471–485.

McConahay, John B. 1983. "Modern Racism and Modern Discrimination: The Effects of Race, Racial Attitudes, and Context on Simulated Hiring Decisions." *Personality and Social Psychology Bulletin* 9 (4): 551–558.

Mayhew, David R. 1991. *Divided We Govern*. New Haven, CT: Yale University.

Mendelberg, Tali. 2001. *The Race Card: Campaign Strategy, Implicit Messages, and the Norm of Equality*. Princeton, NJ: Princeton University Press.

Miller, Nicholas R. 1983. "Pluralism and Social Choice." *American Political Science Review* 77 (3): 734–747.

Miller, Warren E., and Donald E. Stokes. 1963. "Constituency Influence in Congress." *American Political Science Review* 57 (1): 45–56.

Mudde, Cas, and Cristóbal Rovira Kaltwasser. 2017. *Populism: A Very Short Introduction*. Oxford, UK: Oxford University Press.

Nie, N. H., S. Verba, and J. R. Petrocik. (2013[1976]). *The Changing American Voter: Enlarged Edition*. Cambridge, MA: Harvard University Press.

Ogburn, William F., and Estelle Hill. 1935. "Income Classes and the Roosevelt Vote in 1932." *Political Science Quarterly* 50 (2): 186–193.

Peters, Gerhard. 1999–2021. "Presidential Election Margins of Victory." In *The American Presidency Project*. Edited by John T. Woolley and Gerhard Peters. Santa Barbara, CA: University of California. https://www.presidency.ucsb.edu/node/323891

Pew Research Report. August 29, 2022. "As Partisan Hostility Grows, Signs of Frustration With the Two-Party System." https://www.pewresearch.org/politics/2022/08/09/as-partisan-hostility-grows-signs-of-frustration-with-the-two-party-system/

Poole, Keith T., and Howard Rosenthal. 1987. "Analysis of Congressional Coalition Patterns: A Unidimensional Spatial Model." *Legislative Studies Quarterly* 12 (1): 55–75.

Poole, Keith T., and Howard Rosenthal. 1997. *Congress: A Political-Economic History of Roll Call Voting*. New York: Oxford University Press on Demand.

Poole, Keith T., and Howard L. Rosenthal. 2011. *Ideology and Congress*. Vol. 1. New Brunswick: Transaction Publishers.

166 REFERENCES

Powell, G. Bingham, Jr., and Guy D. Whitten. 1993. "A Cross-National Analysis of Economic Voting: Taking Account of the Political Context." *American Journal of Political Science* 21 (3): 391–414.

Rabushka, A., & Shepsle, K. 1972. *Politics in Plural Societies*. Columbus, OH: Charles E. Merrill.

Rae, Douglas W., and Michael Taylor. 1970. *The Analysis of Political Cleavages*. New Haven, CT: Yale University Press.

Riker, William H. 1982. *Liberalism against Populism*. Vol. 34. San Francisco, CA: W. H. Freeman.

Rohde, David W. 1991. *Parties and Leaders in the Postreform House*. Chicago, IL: University of Chicago Press, .

Rosenthal, Howard. 1992. "The Unidimensional Congress Is Not the Result of Selective Gatekeeping." *American Journal of Political Science* 36 (1): 31–35.

Sears, David O. 1988. "Symbolic Racism." In *Eliminating Racism: Profiles in Controversy*, edited by P. A. Katz and D. A. Taylor, 53–84. Boston, MA: Springer US.

Stouffer, Samuel Andrew. 1955. *Communism, Conformity, and Civil Liberties: A Cross-Section of the Nation Speaks Its Mind*. Garden City: Doubleday.

Stokes, Donald E. 1966. "Some Dynamic Elements of Contests for the Presidency." *American Political Science Review* 60 (1): 19–28.

Stokes, Donald E., Angus Campbell, and Warren E. Miller. 1958. "Components of Electoral Decision." *American Political Science Review* 52 (2): 367–387.

Stokes, Donald E., and Warren E. Miller. 1962. "Party Government and the Saliency of Congress." *Public Opinion Quarterly* 26 (4): 531–546.

Taber, Charles S., and Milton Lodge. 2006. "Motivated Skepticism in the Evaluation of Political Beliefs." *American Journal of Political Science* 50 (3): 755–769.

Tappin, Ben M., Gordon Pennycook, and David G. Rand. 2020. "Thinking Clearly about Causal Inferences of Politically Motivated Reasoning: Why Paradigmatic Study Designs Often Undermine Causal Inference." *Current Opinion in Behavioral Sciences* 34: 81–87.

Tate, Katherine. 1994. *From Protest to Politics: The New Black Voters in American Elections*. Cambridge, MA: Harvard University Press.

Taylor, Michael, and Douglas Rae. 1969. "An Analysis of Crosscutting Between Political Cleavages." *Comparative Politics* 1 (4): 534–547.

Theriault, Sean. 2008. *Party Polarization in Congress*. New York: Cambridge University Press.

Theriault, Sean M. 2013. *The Gingrich Senators: The Roots of Partisan Warfare in Congress*. Oxford, UK: Oxford University Press.

Tibbitts, Clark. 1931. "Majority Votes and the Business Cycle." *American Journal of Sociology* 36 (4): 596–606.

Tingley, Dustin, Teppei Yamamoto, Kosuke Hirose, Luke Keele, and Kosuke Imai. 2020. "Mediation: Causal Mediation Analysis." R package, version 4.5.0, CRAN. https://cran.r-project.org/web/packages/mediation/vignettes/mediation.pdf.

Time Staff. June 16, 2015. "Here's Donald Trump's Presidential Announcement Speech." http://time.com/3923128/donald-trump-announcement-speech/.

Truman, David Bicknell. 1951. *The Governmental Process: Political Interests and Public Opinion*. New York: Alfred A. Knopf, Inc.

Tufte, Edward R. 1978. *Political Control of the Economy*. Princeton, NJ: Princeton University Press.

REFERENCES 167

Tversky, Amos, and Daniel Kahneman. 1986. "The Framing of Decisions and the Evaluation of Prospects." *Studies in Logic and the Foundations of Mathematics* 114:503–520.

US Bureau of Economic Analysis. 2023. Real Gross Domestic Product. [A191RO1Q156NBEA]. Federal Reserve Bank of St. Louis. November 27. https://fred.stlouisfed.org/series/A191RO1Q156NBEA, .

Vaillancourt, Pauline Marie. 1973. "Stability of Children's Survey Responses." *Public Opinion Quarterly* 37 (3): 373–387.

von Neumann, John, and Oskar Morganstern. 1944. *Theory of Games and Economic Behavior*. Princeton, NJ: Princeton University Press.

Woodruff, Judy, and Frank Carlson. 2023. "Examining How U.S. Politics Became Intertwined with Personal Identity." *PBS News Hour*, aired March 8, 6:35 p.m. https://www.pbs.org/newshour/show/examining-how-u-s-politics-became-intertwined-with-personal-identity.

Zitner, Aaron, 2023. "Why Tribalism Took Over Our Politics: Social Science Gives an Uncomfortable Explanation: Our Brains Were Made for Conflict." *Wall Street Journal*, August 26. https://www.wsj.com/politics/why-tribalism-took-over-our-politics-5936f48e.

Index

For the benefit of digital users, indexed terms that span two pages (e.g., 52–53) may, on occasion, appear on only one of those pages.

Tables and figures are indicated by *t* and *f* following the page number

Abramowitz, Alan I., 76
Access Hollywood video, 101–3, 102*f*, 102*t*
Achen, Christopher H., 36
ACME (average causal mediation
    effect), 113–15
affective partisanship, 22–23, 144n.4
    candidate assessments, 3, 86–88,
        95–96, 96*f*, 103–5, 104*f*, 113, 140,
        152n.1, 153n.4
    extremism, 124
    growth of, 10–22, 31–32, 86, 87*f*
    substance and emotion, 10–11, 23, 31,
        84, 159n.27
Affordable Care Act (Obamacare), 26
Aldrich, John H., 36–37, 100
American Medical Association, 26
American National Election Study
    (ANES), 5, 11–12, 13–14, 19–20,
        25, 26–27, 41, 42–43, 44, 56–57, 60,
        67–68, 85, 89, 93–94, 100, 101, 105–
        6, 121, 131, 143–44n.12, 144n.13,
        145n.12, 145n.13, 145n.14, 146n.19,
        146n.26, 147–48n.2, 150n.22,
        152n.18, 153n.7, 153n.11
American Political Science Association, 123
American Voter, The (Campbell et al.), 15–
    16, 18, 20, 23–24, 25–26, 27, 44–46,
    45*f*, 52, 109–10, 147n.33
anti-immigration sentiment, 100–1, 102*t*,
    102*f*, 103, 154n.24, 155n.27, 155n.29
Arrow, Kenneth J., 127–29
Articles of Confederation, 16–17, 125–26
average causal mediation effect
    (ACME), 113–15

Baron, Reuben M., 110–12, 114*f*, 115

Bartels, Larry M., 36
Biden, Joseph R. "Joe," Jr., 36–37, 104–5
bipartisanship, 66–67, 104, 119–20, 146–
    47n.31, 154n.19
Bush, George H. W., 28–29, 94, 95–96, 95*f*,
    96*f*, 98*f*
Bush, George W., 117
Bush, John E. "Jeb," 154n.19

Campbell, Angus, 4–5, 9–10, 15–16,
    18–19, 20–22, 23–24, 27, 38, 39–40,
    41–42, 43, 45, 47, 50, 55, 76, 86–89,
    113, 120–21, 123, 132
candidate assessments and evaluations,
    94–103, 140. *See also* affective
    partisanship
    importance of, 88–89
    party identification and, 46, 46*f*
    polarization, 95–96, 96*f*
    role of fundamentals in general
        presidential election, 99–103
    role of fundamentals in presidential
        primary season, 94–99, 154n.17
candidate traits
    effect on voting, 105–12, 107*f*, 109*f*, 110*f*
    mediating the role of fundamentals,
        109–12, 111*f*, 113–15, 114*f*
Cannon, Joseph G., 141
Carson, Jamie L., 89–90
Carter, James E. "Jimmy," 94–97, 95*f*, 96*f*,
    97*f*, 149n.14, 154n.16, 154n.18
Civil Rights Act, 29–30, 118–19, 146n.28
civil rights movement, 29–30, 45, 138–39
Civil War, 27–28, 126
class identity, 17–19, 45
Clean Air and Clean Water Acts, 119

170 INDEX

cleavages, 1–2. *See also* negative affect
  act (behavioral) cleavages, 130
  cognitive dissonance, 34
  crosscutting, 2–3, 11, 16–17, 22, 78–79,
    124–25, 126, 127–29, 132–34, 135*f*,
    138, 140–41
  crystallization, 130, 132, 158n.24
  European multi-party democratic
    systems, 128–29
  fragmentation, 130, 132–33
  growing importance of
    fundamentals, 2–3
  intensity of fragmentation, 130
  Madison's argument in favor of many
    crosscutting cleavages, 126, 127–28
  measures of, 130–31
  measuring with fundamentals, 131–32
  opinion cleavages, 130
  reinforcing, 1–3, 12, 16–17, 34, 56–57,
    78–79, 84, 125, 126, 128–29, 130–31,
    134, 135–37
  risk of democratic backsliding, 141
  stability of democratic institutions, 11,
    16–17, 125–29, 140–41
  trait cleavages, 130
climate change, 34
Clinton, William J. "Bill," 6, 26, 72,
  156–57n.2
Clinton, Hillary R., 12, 13, 94–95, 95*f*, 96*f*,
  97*f*, 99, 101–3, 104–6
cluster sampling, 153n.7
cognition, 10–11, 23, 86–88,
  152n.1, 153n.4
cognitive dissonance, 33–34
Cold War, 119–20
Columbia University, 17–18
Comparative Study of Electoral Systems
  (CSES), 101
congressional elections, 7–8
  1952, 15, 21–22, 88–89
  1954, 15
  1956, 15
  1980, 39
  1984, 58–59, 91
  1994, 117
  2000, 54–55
  2012, 91

  2016, 58–59, 91
  2020, 58–59
  candidate characteristics, 4
  economic retrospection, 35–36
  effect of fundamentals on, 47–50, 49*f*,
    58–59, 59*f*, 139
  familiarity, 89–90, 91, 92*f*, 93*f*
  growing role of fundamentals in, 90–93
  incumbency, 4, 7–8, 7*f*, 58–59, 89–90,
    91, 92*f*, 93*f*, 144n.2
  nationalization of (convergence of
    House and presidential contests), 2,
    8, 10, 53–54, 73
  party identification, 4, 5–6
  split-ticket voting, 8, 9*f*
  turning point in 1984, 1–2, 4, 7–8, 56–
    57, 137, 138
congressional polarization, 10, 62–69, 64*f*,
  74–81, 75*f*, 150n.2
  forming centrist majorities, 66–67, 66*f*
  forming party majorities, 64–66, 65*f*
  ideological dimension, 63–64
  party divergence on fundamentals, 81–
    82, 82*f*, 83*f*, 152n.18
  public perceptions of, 64, 67–69, 68*f*
Converse, Philip E., 4–5, 22, 23–25, 26, 40,
  41–42, 50, 68
COVID-19 pandemic, 34, 51
Cruz, Ted, 94–95, 95*f*, 96*f*, 98*f*, 154n.21
CSES (Comparative Study of Electoral
  Systems), 101

Dawson, Michael C., 31
Democratic Party and Democrats. *See
  also* candidate assessments and
  evaluations; congressional elections;
  presidential elections; *names of
  specific Democrats and fundamentals*
  bipartisanship, 119–20
  conservative coalition, 141–42, 150n.2
  New Deal, 17–18, 141
  progressive versus moderate wings, 142
  Reagan Democrats, 143n.6, 157n.7
  southern Democrats, 27–28, 39, 67,
    117–18, 127, 138–39, 141–42, 156n.1,
    157n.4, 157n.7
  truth value of facts, 34

INDEX   171

Dole, Robert J., 6, 94, 95*f*, 96*f*, 98*f*
DW-Nominate, 63–64, 151n.5, 152n.19

economic retrospection, 9–10, 20, 32–38,
    37*f*, 145n.13, 147–48n.2, 150n.1
  biases and heuristics in decision-
    making, 34–35, 147n.32
  economic-style rational choice, 34–35
  effect of, on voting, 48*f*, 49*f*, 51
  incumbency, 36, 147n.34
  measuring cleavages with, 131–32
  motivated reasoning and cognitive
    dissonance, 33–34, 37–38
  narrow self-interest and pocketbook
    voting, 32, 35
  overall economy, 32–33, 35
  partisan differentiation over most
    important economic measures, 32–33
  perceptions and reality, 36, 37–38, 37*f*
  personal economic anxiety and, 100
  predicting congressional elections,
    91–93, 93*f*
  public polarization, 71*f*, 72–73, 72*f*,
    151n.10
  retrospective voting, 36, 37–38
  role in presidential primary season, 94–
    95, 95*f*, 96–97, 97*f*, 98–99
Eisenhower, Dwight D., 15, 18, 30–31, 88–
    89, 103–4, 119
Electoral College, 2, 127
Erikson, Robert S., 35–36
European multi-party democratic systems,
    128–29, 158nn.20–22
extremism, 2–3, 39–40, 63, 70–72, 74, 83–
    84, 124. *See also* polarization

fake news, 34
familiarity, 89–90
  decreasing role of, 91
  fundamentals and, 91–93, 92*f*, 93*f*
Federalist No. 10 (Madison), 3, 11, 16–
    17, 125–26
Federal Reserve Board, 36–37
Festinger, Leon, 33–34
Fiorina, Morris P., 36, 76
Ford, Gerald R., 67, 149n.14
Freedom Caucus, 67, 142

fundamentals of electoral choice, 9–10.
    See also economic retrospection;
    ideology; issues; party identification
    and partisanship; racial attitudes and
    resentment
  affective polarization, 103–5, 104*f*
  candidate traits and, 105–12, 107*f*, 109*f*
  changes from 1950s to 1970s, 44–46
  criteria for, 19–20
  defined, 19, 144n.9
  direct (total) effect on voting, 47–50,
    48*f*, 49*f*, 145n.11
  funnel of causality model, 45*f*, 45–46, 47
  growing importance and effect of, 2–3,
    4, 5–6, 8, 9, 47–52, 60, 116, 120–23,
    124, 139
  growing number of, 40–44, 120–23, 124
  increasing alignment and reinforcing
    nature of, 12, 51–52, 78–81, 80*f*,
    116, 132–37
  long-term forces, 15–16, 18–19
  measures qualifying as, 9–10, 19, 20
  measuring with crosscutting
    cleavages, 131–32
  party identification and
    partisanship, 15–16
  role in congressional elections, 90–93,
    92*f*, 93*f*
  role in general presidential
    elections, 99–103
  role in presidential primary seasons,
    94–103, 95*f*, 97*f*
  sorting, 2–3, 10, 16, 76–81, 77*f*
  total (pair-wise) effect on voting, 47–50,
    48*f*, 49*f*, 149n.16
  unidimensionality, 120–23, 122*f*
funnel of causality model, 45–46, 45*f*, 47

Gallup, 84–85, 144n.1
general possibility theorem, 127–28
Gingrich, Newt, 67
Goldwater, Barry M., 29, 30–31, 103–4,
    118–19, 146n.28
Gramm, Phil, 147n.1
Great Depression, 36, 127, 141–42
Great Recession, 36–37, 100, 151n.10
Great Society, 26, 29, 118

172 INDEX

Gurin, Gerald, 20–22

Hartwig, Frederick, 45–46
healthcare, government provision of, 26–27, 33–34, 150n.24, 150n.26
Horton, Willie, 28–29
Humphrey, Hubert H., 15

ideology, 9–10, 20, 23–25, 40–44, 145n.10, 146n.19
    absence of shared ideological framework, 24–25
    changes from 1950s to 1970s, 45–46
    decline in extent of crosscutting cleavages, 132–34, 133*f*, 135*f*
    effect of on voting, 48*f*, 49*f*, 50
    as fundamental force, 25, 41, 148n.6
    ideological awareness and understanding, 25, 43, 146n.21, 149n.12
    ideological innocence, 23–24, 41, 43, 45
    liberal-conservative dimension, 23–24, 68, 131–32, 151n.8
    measuring cleavages with, 131–32
    meeting conditions for ideology-related voting, 42–44, 43*f*, 60–61, 139
    party divergence, 82*f*
    party-ideology correlation, 23, 25, 40–41, 78–79, 148n.3
    predicting congressional elections, 90–93, 92*f*, 93*f*
    public polarization, 70*f*, 71*f*, 73, 74, 75*f*
    public's view of congressional polarization, 68–69
    role in presidential primary seasons, 94–95, 95*f*, 96–97, 97*f*, 98–99
    sorting, 77*f*, 78–79, 80*f*
Imai, Kosuke, 110–12, 113
incumbency, 4, 6–8, 7*f*, 58–59, 89–90, 143n.5, 144n.2, 153n.9
    affective polarization, 104
    decreasing role of, 91
    economic retrospection, 36, 147n.34
    fundamentals and, 91–93, 92*f*, 93*f*
isolationism, 119–20
issues, 9–10, 20, 25–27, 41–44, 145n.10, 145n.12, 152n.1
    changes from 1950s to 1970s, 45–46

decline in extent of crosscutting cleavages, 132–34, 133*f*, 135*f*
defense spending, 26–27
effect of on voting, 48*f*, 49*f*, 50
four-issue scale of voting criteria, 42–43, 44, 149n.10
as fundamental force, 26, 42–43
government services, 26–27
growth in issue-related voting, 26, 27, 42–43, 43*f*, 44, 46, 46*f*
healthcare, 26
jobs and standard of living, 26–27
liberal-conservative dimension, 26, 131–32
measuring cleavages with, 131–32
meeting conditions for issue-related voting, 25–27, 42–43, 43*f*, 60–61, 139
minority group aid, 26–27
party divergence, 82*f*
predicting congressional elections, 90–93, 92*f*, 93*f*
public polarization, 70*f*, 71*f*, 73, 74, 75*f*
sorting, 77*f*, 78, 80*f*
Iyengar, Shanto, 86

Jacobson, Gary C., 7, 8, 89–90
Jardina, Ashley, 31–32
Jim Crow system, 27–28, 45, 117, 118, 127, 138–39, 141, 142
Johnson, Lyndon B., 26, 29, 30–31, 103–4, 118

Kahneman, Daniel, 34–35
Kalmoe, Nathan P., 24–25
Kelly, Megyn, 101
Kennedy, Edward M. "Ted," 94–96, 95*f*, 96*f*, 97*f*
Kennedy, John F., 15
Kenny, David A., 110–12, 114*f*, 115
Kinder, Donald R., 24–25
Korean War, 45
Kramer, Gerald H., 35–36, 37–38

Lazarsfeld, Paul F., 17–18, 53
Levendusky, Matthew, 76
liberal-conservative dimension
    ideology, 23–24, 68, 131–32, 151n.8

INDEX 173

issues, 26, 131–32
Lijphart, Arend, 129
Lipset, Seymour Martin, 11

MacKuen, Michael B., 35–36
Madison, James, 3, 11, 16–17, 125–26, 140–41
March on Washington, 29–30
Mason, Lilliana, 86
Mayhew, David R., 124
McCarthy era, 45
McGovern, George S., 15, 103–4
Medicaid, 26
Medicare, 26
Miller, Nicholas R., 127–28
Miller, Warren E., 4–5, 20–22, 27–28, 58–59, 88–89
modern sexism, 101, 102f, 102t

nationalization of elections (convergence of House and presidential contests), 2, 8, 10, 53–54, 73
National Science Foundation (NSF), 13, 143n.10, 143–44n.12, 153n.11
negative affect, 22–23, 86–88, 144n.4
   candidate assessments, 3, 86–88, 95–96, 96f, 103–5, 104f, 113, 140, 152n.1, 153n.4
   extremism, 124
   growth of, 10–22, 31–32, 86, 87f
   substance and emotion, 10–11, 23, 31, 84, 159n.27
New Deal, 15, 17–18, 29, 119–42
Nixon, Richard M., 15, 103–4, 119
NSF (National Science Foundation), 13, 143n.10, 143–44n.12, 153n.11

Obama, Barack, 36–37, 51, 72, 133, 150n.23
Obamacare (Affordable Care Act), 26
O'Neill, Thomas P. "Tip," Jr., 7, 89, 143n.3

party identification and partisanship, 3, 4–6, 9–11, 20–23, 150n.21, 152n.20
   African-American party identification shift, 29–31, 29f, 30f
   candidate assessments and, 88–89
   candidate traits and, 108–9

   changes from 1950s to 1970s, 45–46
   as core or tribal identity, 22
   decline in extent of crosscutting cleavages, 132–34, 133f, 135f
   declining effect of, 46, 46f, 50, 51
   defecting to vote against their party's candidates, 39–40
   early formation and durability of, 15–16, 22, 40, 145nn.16–17, 146n.29
   effect of on voting, 47, 48f, 49f, 50
   emergence and overlapping of other fundamental forces, 16, 51–52
   as fundamental force, 15–16f
   funnel of causality model, 45f
   leaners, 20–21, 50, 131
   measuring, 20–21
   measuring cleavages with, 131
   most important economic measures, 32–33
   negative affect, 22
   party-ideology correlation, 23, 25, 40–41, 78–79
   predicting congressional elections, 90–93, 92f, 93f
   public polarization, 70f, 71f, 73, 74, 75f, 84–85
   pure Independents, 21
   racial, ethnic, and social identity, 31–32
   role in presidential primary seasons, 94–95, 95f, 96–97, 97f, 98–99
   seven-point scale, 19, 20–21
   as single long-term attitude of importance, 16, 24, 40
   sorting, 78–79, 80f
   substance of politics, 22
   White fear of becoming a minority, 32
   White party identification shift, 29f, 30f
   winning elections versus, 15, 21–22
party sorting. *See* sorting
PCA (principal components analysis), 121–23, 157n.12
person-perception, 105–6
Pew, 85
PIP3 model, 56, 57–58, 57f, 79–81, 80f, 90–91, 92f, 107, 109f, 121, 122–23, 122f, 131–33, 134, 135–37, 157n.9. *See also* ideology; issues; party identification and partisanship

174 INDEX

PIPER model, 56, 57, 57*f*, 79–81, 80*f*, 90–91, 93*f*, 107, 121, 122–23, 122*f*, 131–32, 134, 135–37, 157n.9. *See also* economic retrospection; ideology; issues; party identification and partisanship; racial attitudes and resentment
polarization, 2–3, 62–85, 116–20
  affective, 103–5, 104*f*
  candidate assessments, 95–96, 96*f*
  congressional, 10, 62–69, 64*f*, 65*f*, 66*f*, 68*f*, 74–82, 75*f*, 82*f*, 83*f*, 121, 136*f*, 138, 150n.2
  economic issues, 32–33
  long-term continuity of, 124
  mid-century call for more, 123
  negative affective partisanship, 10–11
  party divergence on fundamentals, 81–82, 82*f*, 83*f*
  public, 2–3, 10, 39–40, 62–63, 69–74, 70*f*, 71*f*, 75*f*, 81–82, 83*f*, 116, 134–37, 136*f*
  sorting, 16, 39–40, 63, 74–81, 77*f*
Poole, Keith T., 63–66, 67–68, 86, 120–21
populism and populist sentiment, 100, 101, 102*f*, 141, 154nn.24–25, 155n.27
presidential elections, 4–6
  1916, 36
  1952, 4–5, 15, 21–22, 88–89
  1956, 4–5, 15, 21–22
  1960, 4–5, 15
  1964, 103–4, 118–19
  1968, 15
  1972, 15, 44, 103–4
  1976, 44
  1980, 39, 44, 72, 93–99, 95*f*, 96*f*, 97*f*, 98*f*
  1984, 58
  1988, 28–29, 73
  1992, 72
  2008, 72
  2012, 51
  2016, 12, 13, 58, 93–103, 95*f*, 96*f*, 97*f*, 98*f*, 102*f*, 104–5, 142
  2020, 50, 58, 142
  candidate assessments, 94–103, 95*f*
  candidate characteristics, 4, 5
  economics and politics, 36–37

effect of fundamentals on, 47–50, 48*f*, 56–58, 57*f*, 139
gyration between close contests and landslides, 4–5, 6*f*
incumbency, 6, 8
nationalization of (convergence of House and presidential contests), 2, 8
party identification, 4–5
social context of voting, 17–18
split-ticket voting, 8, 9*f*
standard deviation of victory margins, 6*f*, 6
turning point in 1984, 1–2, 4, 5–6, 56–57, 137, 138
principal components analysis (PCA), 121–23, 157n.12
public polarization, 2–3, 10, 39–40, 62–63, 69–74, 70*f*, 71*f*, 75*f*, 81–82, 83*f*, 116, 134–37, 136*f*

racial attitudes and resentment, 9–10, 17–19, 20, 27–32, 145n.14, 150n.1
  African-American party identification shift, 29–31, 29*f*, 30*f*
  civil rights movement, 27–28, 29–30
  coded new racism language, 28–29
  effect of on voting, 48*f*, 49*f*, 51
  growing role of, 51–52
  as historical fundamental force, 27–28
  measuring cleavages with, 131–32
  party divergence, 82*f*
  predicting congressional elections, 91–93, 93*f*
  public polarization, 70*f*, 70–72, 71*f*, 73, 74, 75*f*
  racial, ethnic, and social identity, 31–32
  role in presidential primary seasons, 99, 154n.23
  sorting, 77*f*, 78, 152n.15
  substance of politics, 31
  White fear of becoming a minority, 32
  White party identification shift, 29–31, 29*f*, 30*f*
Reagan, Ronald, 39, 72, 94, 95*f*, 96*f*, 98*f*, 117, 119–20, 143n.6, 154n.16, 154n.18

INDEX   175

Reconstruction, 27–28, 63–64, 117, 118, 127
religion, 17–19, 144n.8, 150n.25
Republican Party and Republicans. *See also* candidate assessments and evaluations; congressional elections; polarization; presidential elections; sorting; *names of specific Republicans and fundamentals*
  bipartisanship, 119–20
  conservative coalition, 150n.2
  emergence of, 27–28, 118
  Freedom Caucus, 67, 142
  Gingrich Republicans, 67
  pre-Depression majority, 127, 138–39, 141–42
  Reconstruction era, 27–28
  Republican revolution, 117
  RINO label, 118–19
  Rockefeller Republicans, 118–19
  Tea Party Republicans, 67, 142
  truth value of facts, 34
Rockefeller, Nelson A., 118–19, 157n.6
Rokkan, Stein, 11
Roosevelt, Franklin D., 17–18, 29, 118
Roosevelt, Theodore, 141
Rosenthal, Howard, 63–66, 67–68, 86, 120–21
Rubio, Marco A., 94–95, 95*f*, 96*f*, 98*f*, 154n.21

Sanders, Bernie, 94–95, 95*f*, 96*f*, 97*f*, 99, 100, 142, 154n.20
Saunders, Kyle L., 76
SES. *See* socioeconomic status
sexism, 101, 102*t*, 102*f*
short-term attitudes, 18, 44, 47, 58, 84, 86–88, 112–13, 139, 140, 149n.16, 153n.5
slavery, 118, 126, 128
social security, 119
socioeconomic status (SES), 52–56
  effect of on voting, 47–50, 52, 53–56, 54*f*, 57, 150n.21, 150n.23
  funnel of causality model, 45*f*
  setting context and shaping of fundamentals, 18–19, 52, 53–56

sorting (party sorting), 2–3, 10, 63, 103–4, 116, 138–40, 157n.7
  debate over, 76
  deck of cards analogy, 74–76
  decline in extent of crosscutting cleavages, 133*f*, 135–37
  effect on fundamentals, 76–81, 77*f*
  fragmentation, 132
  ideology, 77*f*, 78–79, 80*f*
  issues, 77*f*, 78, 80*f*
  party identification and partisanship, 78–79, 80*f*
  polarization, 16, 39–40, 63, 74–81, 77*f*
  racial attitudes and resentment, 77*f*, 78
  reinforcing cleavages, 15–16
  southern Democrats and Rockefeller Republicans, 117–19, 120
stagflation, 45
Stimson, James A., 35–36
Stokes, Donald E., 4–5, 10–11, 27–28, 58–59, 60, 88–89, 105, 109–10, 112–13
surveys
  ANES, 5, 11–12, 13–14
  continuity, 13–14
  reasons for use of, 12–13
  sampling, 13
  scrutiny of and controversy over, 12

Taft, William Howard, 141
Tea Party, 67, 142
Tingley, Dustin, 113
Trump, Donald J., 12, 13, 36–37, 53–54, 94–95, 95*f*, 96*f*, 98–99, 98*f*, 100–3, 102*t*, 104–6, 120–21, 143n.7, 154n.20
Tversky, Amos, 34–35
tyrannies, 11, 16–17, 125–26, 127–28, 141, 142, 158n.18

unidimensionality, 120–23, 122*f*, 125, 158n.13

vaccine politics, 34
Vietnam War, 45, 119–20, 145n.12
Voting Rights Act, 29–30, 118

Wallace, George C., 15, 28
War on Poverty, 26, 29, 118
Wilson, Woodrow, 36

The manufacturer's authorised representative in the EU for product safety is
Oxford University Press España S.A. of el Parque Empresarial San Fernando
de Henares, Avenida de Castilla, 2 – 28830 Madrid (www.oup.es/en).

Printed in the USA/Agawam, MA
December 13, 2024

878851.015